Taking the Mystery Out of

TQM

A Practical Guide to Total Quality Management

By
Peter Capezio and Debra Morehouse

CAREER PRESS
180 Fifth Avenue
P.O. Box 34
Hawthorne, NJ 07507
1-800-CAREER-1
201-427-0229 (outside U.S.)
FAX: 201-427-2037

TAKING THE MYSTERY OUT OF TQM
A PRACTICAL GUIDE TO TOTAL QUALITY MANAGEMENT
ISBN 1-56414-105-5, $16.95
Cover design by Dean Johnson Design, Inc.
Printed in the U.S.A. by Book-mart Press

To order this title by mail, please include price as noted above, $2.50 handling per order, and $1.00 for each book ordered. Send to: Career Press, Inc., 180 Fifth Ave., P.O. Box 34, Hawthorne, NJ 07507

Or call toll-free 1-800-CAREER-1 (Canada: 201-427-0229) to order using VISA or MasterCard, or for further information on books from Career Press.

Library of Congress Cataloging-in-Publication Data

Capezio, Peter, 1947-
   Taking the mystery out of TQM : a practical guide to total quality management / by Peter Capezio and Debra Morehouse.
     p. cm.
   ISBN 1-56414-105-5 : $16.95
   1. Total quality management. I. Morehouse, Debra L. II. Title.
HD62. 15.C35   1993
658.5'62--dc20

                                  93-24301
                                      CIP

Acknowledgments

Authors

Peter J. Capezio
Debra L. Morehouse

Special Thanks to

Rodney Matheson
Doreen Walker

The authors wish to acknowledge Wendell Leimbach, AME Group, for an orientation to total quality and its benefits, and Steve Johnson, Praxis Associates, for his thoughts on paradigms and charts reflecting continuous improvement.

Legend Symbol Guide

 Checklist that will help you identify important issues for future application.

 Exercises that reinforce your learning experience.

 Questions that will help you apply the critical points to your situation.

Examples that clarify and illustrate important points.

Example

Real-world case studies that will help you apply the information you've learned.

C
A
S
E

S
T
U
D
Y

Legend Symbol Guide (continued)

Key issues to learn and understand for future application.

Quick refresher of the main issues.

CONTENTS

Contents

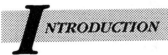

*I*NTRODUCTION

The Road of
Continuous Improvement . . .

In today's competitive business environment, companies are being challenged to improve performance by continuously improving processes, cutting costs and increasing output. These changes mean going beyond the traditional management systems and creating a culture — an attitude toward continuous improvement, with a focus on both a company's internal and external customers.

The focus of Total Quality Management (TQM) will center on you as an individual and on your company to help you utilize total quality principles to understand customer requirements and do things right the first time. In essence, TQM is a process and a way of thinking for doing business now and in the future. TQM companies in virtually every industry are emerging as the leaders of tomorrow.

Some key considerations discussed in this manual include:

What is TQM and what are its benefits?

What does TQM mean to you as a manager or supervisor?

How can you assess the TQM readiness of both yourself and your company?

How can TQM improve your performance?

How do TQM companies work?

> *"Quality is a journey, not a destination."*
>
> **David K. Carr**

> *"The spirit of this organization is the business of every one of us."*
>
> *Peter F. Drucker*

Some key questions that will be answered include:

Can one person make a difference?

Where do you start?

What's in it for you?

Why change now?

One person can make a difference. TQM is a powerful process to help you manage change and influence all the people with whom you work. Just think about working in a company where employees understand not only how to do their jobs right, but also how to improve their jobs and work processes significantly on a regular basis. That's TQM at work!

_C_HAPTER 1

Total Quality Management (TQM)

WHAT IS TQM?

Total Quality Management refers to a management process and set of disciplines that are coordinated to ensure that the organization consistently meets and exceeds customer requirements. TQM engages all divisions, departments and levels of the organization. Top management organizes all of its strategy and operations around customer needs and develops a culture with high employee participation. TQM companies are focused on the systematic management of data in all processes and practices to eliminate waste and pursue continuous improvement.

The goal is to deliver the highest value for the customer at the lowest cost while achieving sustained profit and economic stability for the company. Top management must commit to a vision and align and train its employees toward a common mission. To do this, cross-functional teams work on improvements that respond to customer requirements. Long-term relationships with customers, suppliers and employees focus on quality beyond short-term profit.

> *QUALITY:*
> *a new way of*
> *thinking, being,*
> *acting, doing.*

TQM alters the way a company thinks about work and all of its relationships as it impacts every function, system and person connected with the company. TQM is a continuous journey toward excellence.

WHAT DOES TQM MEAN TO YOU?

As managers and supervisors, you are on the front lines of innovation in business and industry today. Top management and the people you direct look to you for guidance in how to make necessary improvements. Small business owners are in the same position in directing their employees. The world of work has changed dramatically from an era when all orders came down from the "top" with a due date. Global competition and advances in technology have created market conditions that make all projects and programs "past due" before they are even out of the gate.

Your job working in or creating a TQM environment is to accept the challenge of delivering innovation and improvements in how your company accomplishes its work. How you understand the needs of your customers — both those inside and outside the company — and how you align and develop resources — both human and technical — to meet customer requirements will make all the difference in your company's success.

It is essential for companies to differentiate between their internal and external customers in making process improvements and achieving quality gains. Internal customers are those people within the company who receive the results of your work. When you need a service, a function performed or a part from another department in your company, you are the internal customer. The efficiency and quality of the responses to internal customers throughout the customer chain influence how well satisfied the external or "ultimate" customer will be. Meeting customer requirements means there is diligence and quality at every step.

Learning the principles and practices of Total Quality Management will help you achieve outstanding results and enlist the support of top management in advancing TQM within the organization. From the level of an area manager or supervisor, you can influence "change at the top" and create a

---

The customer redefined:

SUPPLIERS

Company Depts.

Internal Customers

EXTERNAL CUSTOMERS

work environment that gets the best from its workers. The proof will be reflected in the results you and your employees deliver to your company's customers.

TQM AWARENESS CHECKLIST

TQM has evolved over the past 50 years and combines management approaches from structural, technical and humanistic frameworks. Probably some of what you and your company already do reflects TQM principles and practices. Rate your company and yourself on TQM applications in the TQM Checklist on a scale from 1 - 5 based on the following criteria. Each item is worth a maximum of five points, with five representing the greatest TQM strength in a given area. The highest possible score you can achieve is 50 (25 points each) in rating TQM readiness for the company and for the managers and supervisors. This checklist will help you and your co-workers determine how active you are in applying TQM principles and practices in your company.

TQM AWARENESS CHECKLIST

Rate each item A-E below according to the scale 1-5 as described here.

RATING SCALE

1   No Awareness/No Application: No awareness of TQM principles and no application

2   Minimal Awareness/Minimal Application: Some awareness, but little application or follow-through in any area or department

3   Evolving Awareness/Some Application: Evolving awareness, and some application and follow-through in an area or department

4   Established Awareness/Some Integration: Established awareness, some application and follow-through, but limited integration and use within the company as a whole

5   Comprehensive Awareness/ Full Integration: Comprehensive awareness and integration of TQM principles and practices throughout the company as a whole

YOUR COMPANY

A.   The mission and goals of the company are clear.   _____

B.   Top management communicates in a timely and purposeful way with employees about the "big picture" — new products, growth, market share, achievements and problems.   _____

C.   The company is driven by quality.   _____

D.   The company is focused on customer needs.   _____

E.   The company provides clear incentives for employees to seek improvements and innovations.   _____

TOTAL COMPANY SCORE   _____
(Highest Possible Score = 25)

TQM AWARENESS CHECKLIST

Rate each item A-E below according to the scale 1-5 as described on the facing page.

MANAGERS/SUPERVISORS IN YOUR COMPANY

A. Active and effective cross-functional teams work on process improvements. _____

B. Communication is open, people are respected and trust is the norm. _____

C. Managers and supervisors regularly initiate new ideas and practices and serve as a positive link between top management and employees. _____

D. Managers and supervisors are committed to developing both themselves and the employees. _____

E. Managers and supervisors work with their employees to create regular avenues for customer interaction and input. _____

TOTAL MANAGERS/SUPERVISORS SCORE _____
(Highest Possible Score = 25)

Interpreting the Results

Now that you have rated the TQM readiness of your company and your managers and supervisors, you have a clearer idea about how well you meet the needs of your customers and how well your company integrates communication, existing operations and systems, as well as about the level of commitment management has to innovation and improvements.

You may be asking, "What can I do as a manager or supervisor to increase TQM awareness and activity in my immediate work environment?" Everyone needs to start somewhere. Frequently, changes to "how the job gets done" come from the part of an organization that has the greatest autonomy in doing the work. That gives managers and supervisors a chance to influence attitudes, values and behaviors.

Today, creative managers and supervisors in American industry are taking on leadership responsibility to introduce TQM principles and practices throughout the productivity chain. They are focused on adding value for customers and saving money for their companies in an ongoing series of small steps. The material in this manual will help you in your goal of becoming a champion in your role as a TQM manager or supervisor.

Review the TQM Awareness Checklist to get a solid picture of how TQM principles are applied in practice. You will find several sections of the book helpful in describing real work situations in companies that practice TQM. Refer especially to sections on:

- "How TQM Practices and Principles Can Improve Your Performance" (Chapter 2)

- "How TQM Companies Work" (Chapter 2)

- "Assessment of TQM Readiness" (Chapter 7)

- "TQM: Organization Culture Change" and "Paradigm Shift" (Chapter 9)

YOUR FIRST RESPONSIBILITY—DEVELOPING PEOPLE

Satisfied employees help create satisfied customers. As a manager or supervisor, the critical mandate in your role as "boss" is to develop your employees to contribute their best. You help create satisfied employees.

The most influential factors for their job satisfaction are mastery of the knowledge and skills essential for doing one's job and development of positive relationships at work. The single most significant relationship in determining "success on the job" is one's relationship to the boss.

As a small-business owner, manager or supervisor, your first responsibility is to guide people in producing the best results possible for the company. You must train and coach people to master the knowledge and skills required to excel in their jobs, and to master your own style of interpersonal communication. When people experience a consistently high rate of job satisfaction, they produce their best work and deliver high quality for their customers. Masterful and recognized employees excel at delighting the customer.

First, understand the vision and mission of your organization. Second, develop a working style and incentives that produce "action steps" among your employees, co-workers and boss. Create customer-driven, high-quality operations and processes. To do this, you must learn about the unique talents and concerns of the people who work with you and for you. Become clear about what motivates them, how each seeks personal-performance improvement and how you can help.

Remember: The best way to get your boss's commitment to TQM is to demonstrate the results of your committed team. The proof is in the pudding. As your team discovers ways to improve quality and reduce costs, it will be recognized for its new TQM practices.

> *Satisfied employees help create satisfied customers.*

> *When people experience a consistently high rate of job satisfaction, they produce their best work and deliver high quality for their customers.*

7

"MANAGING UP": GETTING "BUY-IN" FROM YOUR BOSS

Frequently, managers and supervisors complain that their bosses do not understand what it takes for them to achieve success. Sometimes bosses themselves are lacking in their own abilities to lead, manage and communicate effectively. However, the fact remains that real work must be accomplished with greater and greater precision and quality. TQM environments require that managers and supervisors learn how to "manage up" in their organizations, as well as to direct and influence the work of subordinates and peers.

Granted, this commitment to manage one's boss looms as a tall order. However, neglecting communication around vital concerns keeps you operating in a vacuum. Early "buy-in" from your boss will make later negotiations for such matters as process improvements and requests for additional resources more obtainable. Finding early agreement on the scope of responsibilities and the definition of success is essential in TQM.

Bosses do not necessarily take the lead in communication, yet the need exists to build alliances. Therefore, front-line managers and supervisors must be willing to develop skills to address this challenge as an essential first step in strengthening their own positions and authority and in developing a TQM culture of high employee participation among their subordinates and co-workers.

Remember: The best way for you to achieve the commitment of your team is to model a collaborative relationship with your boss. Employees will model the process they witness between you and your boss. If the norm above them is one of open communication and respect, then workers will feel safe to operate in the same way.

CHAPTER 2

How TQM Companies Work

QUALITY AND VALUE ARE WHAT THE CUSTOMER PERCEIVES THEM TO BE

Companies that subscribe to Total Quality Management focus their strategy, their operations and their employees around "listening to the customer." Understanding who makes up the customer base and the various market segments within that base provides companies with the best clues about market share, resources for growth and market needs. The following characteristics differentiate TQM companies from those with more traditional practices that threaten their existence.

> *"What is our business?" is not determined by the producer but by the consumer."*
>
> *Peter F. Drucker*

9

TQM Companies	Traditional Companies
Customer-driven	Company-driven
Total customer service	Customer satisfaction less than 100%
Long-term commitment	Short-term profitability
Continuous improvement	High-cost production and waste
Elimination of waste	High scrap and rework
High quality and low cost	Low quality and high cost
Quality at the source	Inspection after the fact
Leading people and measuring variance	Rating people and measuring performance
Cross-functional teams	Fortressed departments
High employee participation	Top-down hierarchy
Multilevel communication	Formal channels of top-down communication

TQM PRINCIPLES IN ACTION: WHERE DO YOU START?

One person can make a difference. An entire company of persons interacting can make a difference. The most effective TQM companies demonstrate TQM principles in the everyday actions and interactions of running the business. Consider how the items on the next five pages correspond to the roles of top management as well as those of managers, supervisors and employee contributors. The list is not intended to be all-inclusive; it will serve as a beginning tool to help you focus on practicing TQM.

After each item, note any barriers you, your department or your company may have that interfere with the practice of these principles. Also, note the supports that exist. Then, go

over each of your comments carefully to see what you can do about it. Name other people who can help or who need to participate. When you are done, you will have identified where you need to begin or improve your own TQM process. Continuous improvement starts with each individual.

HOW TQM COMPANIES WORK

Top Management

1. Customer-driven vision and shared values are communicated throughout the organization to deliver high-quality and low-cost products and services.

   Barriers/Supports: _____
   _____
   _____

   What Can I Do? / Who Else Can Help? _____
   _____
   _____

2. Trust, open communication and mutual respect are nurtured and rewarded.

   Barriers/Supports: _____
   _____
   _____

   What Can I Do? / Who Else Can Help? _____
   _____
   _____

Top Management (continued)

3. Broad expectations are established at the top and for your department; creativity, innovation, and research and development are stimulated and rewarded.

    Barriers/Supports: _____

    _____

    _____

    What Can I Do? / Who Else Can Help? _____

    _____

    _____

4. The top level is committed to TQM by valuing quality and learning more than schedule and profit.

    Barriers/Supports: _____

    _____

    _____

    What Can I Do? / Who Else Can Help? _____

    _____

    _____

Managers, Supervisors and Employee Contributors

1. Leadership in developing improvement processes through cross-functional teams and the integration of technology and the control (measurement) of systems is encouraged.

    Barriers/Supports: _____
    _____
    _____

    What Can I Do? / Who Else Can Help? _____
    _____
    _____

2. Customer requirements including conformance, continuous improvement and total customer satisfaction are developed.

    Barriers/Supports: _____
    _____
    _____

    What Can I Do? / Who Else Can Help? _____
    _____
    _____

Managers, Supervisors and Employee Contributors (continued)

3.   Training in TQM principles and tools — meeting customer
     requirements, measuring results along the road of continuous
     improvement, creative and strategic thinking and planning,
     problem-solving, resolving conflict, working in teams — is initiated.

     Barriers/Supports: _____

     _____

     _____

     What Can I Do? / Who Else Can Help? _____

     _____

     _____

4.   "Best Practices" of best companies are benchmarked.

     Barriers/Supports: _____

     _____

     _____

     What Can I Do? / Who Else Can Help? _____

     _____

     _____

Managers, Supervisors and Employee Contributors (continued)

5.   Work teams and process flows adjust to new product/service
       requirements.

       Barriers/Supports: _____

       _____

       _____

       What Can I Do? / Who Else Can Help? _____

       _____

       _____

6.   Sole-source suppliers model TQM principles to serve end-user
       needs.

       Barriers/Supports: _____

       _____

       _____

       What Can I Do? / Who Else Can Help? _____

       _____

       _____

**Select any of these items that top management, managers, supervisors
and employees must develop as initial steps in the TQM process. Use
them as points of discussion and key objectives.**

WHAT COMPANIES ARE SAYING ABOUT TQM

It is not through technology alone that TQM has made its impression on those gauging the industrial prowess of the Japanese over the past 45 years, as well as the more recent achievements of American total-quality companies. It is precisely the blend of statistical and technical processes — along with human-management technology — that makes many believe that this time of "interactive" ideologies is unique. Now there is an opportunity to bring to the forefront the advantage of many ways of knowing and to harness those "learnings" into integrated, intelligent and global ways of doing things. TQM seems to offer this opportunity.

In TQM, art and science meet and meld. The hard sciences synergize with the social sciences. Through TQM, W. Edwards Deming's concept of "profound knowledge" comes to life — when systems thinking is applied to both machines and processes and organizations and people. East meets West and right-brain/left-brain know-how stimulate each other to create a whole that is greater than the sum of its parts.

Whether one believes TQM really represents such a holistic approach, as does Deming, or sees TQM as a means to get control of managing quality in products and services, as does Joseph M. Juran, one thing does appear to be true: TQM works.

Companies run better. Customers remain loyal because they are satisfied with the responsiveness of companies to their needs. Companies develop high-performance, cross-functional teams. Institutional learning is captured. You collect data, analyze it and use it to make continuous process improvements. Companies invest in training and measure the value of the training by assessing its impact in the workplace. Suppliers and unions buy in; and productivity and quality continue to improve at lower cost for the customer.

Some say the homogeneity of the Japanese culture promotes the success of TQM, whereas the diversity and heterogeneity of the U.S. culture makes TQM difficult if not impossible. For sure, America is on an irreversible journey to discover the answer to this most serious question.

> *"Traditional American management tolerates errors and waste if these do not exceed standards and specifications."*
>
> *Ian D. Littman*

16

In a recent survey, 250 leading U.S. companies were asked what strategies they were using, if any, to address the issues of quality and continuous improvement. The following reflects which strategies the companies are using and what percentage of the companies have implemented specific efforts. The vast majority reported that evaluation was ongoing and beneficial to demonstrating progress for the company in areas of key concern.

Quality and Improvement Strategies of U.S. Companies

Customer Satisfaction	87%
Employee Involvement	86%
TQM	68%
Benchmarking	60%
Supplier Partnerships	58%
Self-Managed Teams	35%

The companies who participate in the Malcolm Baldrige National Quality Award have encouraging reports. They explain TQM is not a "quick fix." There is no recipe or roadmap. A weekend course — or a month-long one — at any of the nation's leading universities will not give you the tool kit you might like. TQM does not come in a box — or even on a video cassette.

Total Quality Management is providing American companies who have committed to TQM with an opportunity to renew or reinvent their corporations from the inside out. Gauge the results of Xerox, Federal Express and IBM for yourself.

TQM is not the project of the month — it is a new, enduring culture.

17

XEROX CORPORATION, STAMFORD, CT
BUSINESS PRODUCTS AND SERVICES DIVISION
1990 Baldrige Winner

Xerox was losing market share rapidly in the early 1980s. In 1980, the Japanese had 20% of the U.S. auto market, but they had 40% of the U.S. copier business. Domestic as well as foreign competitors were surpassing Xerox in reprographic products in both cost and quality. Xerox was in crisis.

In 1984, Xerox launched an ambitious program of "Leadership Through Quality." The company invested $125 million in training over the next five years. Every employee received 28 hours of training in problem-solving and improvement techniques at the beginning of the training program.

When Xerox first began its search for "how" to begin with TQM, they paid to hear all the quality gurus and spoke with other corporations using TQM. What they heard — and what Xerox learned from its experience — is that each organization has to create its own strategy and develop a plan with its people that fits its culture.

Xerox came up with four core principles for its corporation. Customer satisfaction stands alone and ranks first in importance. The other three are equal in importance to each other: achieving projected return on assets, increasing market share and maintaining a dedicated workforce.

Xerox identified these core values:

- Success through customer satisfaction
- Deliver quality and excellence in all things
- Maintain a premium return on assets
- Acquire the technology to develop marketplace leadership
- Develop employees to their fullest potential
- Act as a responsible corporate citizen

> *CUSTOMER SATISFACTION stands alone and ranks first in importance.*

Xerox also named six enablers to produce Quality:

- Behavioral change for senior management
- Transition teams
- Training
- Modification of the reward and recognition system
- New communication patterns and norms
- Tools and processes

Xerox used these tools in developing its "Leadership Through Quality" program:

- Communication and problem-solving training
- Benchmarking
- Calculating the cost of nonconformance
- Measurements of quality (products and processes)
- Management by fact (data collection and analysis)
- Mapping each process to create a "seamless" organization

Former CEO David Kearns was active throughout and assumed the leadership role with both integrity and pizazz. He made quality improvement and customer satisfaction the job of every employee. Today, salaried and hourly employees are expected to solve problems and improve product quality and customer service.

Xerox sends out monthly surveys to 55,000 Xerox equipment owners. From the responses, Xerox learns what owners need and want and what they will pay to get the conveniences and features that will mean the most to them. Xerox then uses the information to plan and develop delivery of what customers want.

Team Xerox has more than 7,000 teams worldwide and says over 75% of its workforce is active on one or more teams. Xerox credits teams with saving $116 million by tightening production cycles, reducing scrap, and devising standards and measures to improve processes.

Emphasis on QUALITY in all facets of XEROX.

19

Xerox credits the following as a direct result of its Quality program:

- 78% decrease in defects per 100 machines
- 20% decrease in service response time
- 40% decrease in rework
- Reductions in labor and overhead material
- Improved quality products and customer loyalty
- **1993 Goals:** 50% reduction in unit manufacturing cost
  Fourfold improvement in reliability

Xerox did extensive benchmarking on 240 key areas of product, service and business performance. "Standards" came from world leaders in each category, regardless of industry.

Xerox's advice to those who will implement TQM:

- TQM is a top-down process; management must lead it.
- The organization will have to "mature" into TQM.
- There will be a change in the company's culture.
- TQM requires discipline and patience; it is not for the superstar leader who will not let go of control or the limelight.
- In TQM, everybody shines; they have to!

When asked if a division could implement TQM without corporate already being involved from the top, Xerox had these thoughts. It may be possible if the division:

- Is fairly self-contained and not interdependent with other divisions
- has been authorized to act fairly autonomously from its corporate office and has the resources to achieve its goals

However, the division focus will eventually compete with the short-term profit focus of the corporation, unless the organization as a whole becomes focused on quality.

IT

ALL

ADDS

UP . . .

20

FEDERAL EXPRESS CORPORATION, MEMPHIS, TN
1990 Baldrige Winner

Federal Express has been aggressive since the beginning.
Fed Ex went the TQM route because it wanted to maintain and
expand market share. Founder and CEO Fred Smith launched
the air express industry in 1973. Within 10 years, Fed Ex was a
$1 billion company. In 1990, it achieved $7 billion in revenue.

**CEO Fred Smith gave TQM full rein and drove the
process.** He was visible and vital throughout and gave
everyone room to participate.

Guiding Principles

- People
- Service
- Profit
- Management by fact and analysis
- Continuous improvement (Deming Cycle and
  philosophy)

Training

Fed Ex is committed to ongoing training and a continuous
focus on improvement. Managers have the responsibility of
training their front-line people. Fed Ex has a worldwide system
for gaining input from teams throughout its network on how
people are being managed and what training people need
most. Morale is also checked; Fed Ex's last report card earned
the company a 91% "I'm proud to be a Fed Ex employee"
rating.

Recognition Program

Fed Ex has an employee-recognition program for both
individual and team successes and contributions. The company
is very active in recognizing people in a routine way to
support continuous improvement.

> *Commitment to
> ongoing training
> and a continuous
> focus on
> improvement.*

21

Fed Ex explains that one of the most telling sources of data the company uses to find out how well it is doing is the Service Quality Indicator (SQI).

SQI is a 12-component, weighted index describing how performance is viewed by the customer. Daily SQI reports are developed from worldwide input. Quality Action Teams (QATs) work on the data each day and utilize 30 databases to locate root causes of customer complaints. Cross-functional teams work in introducing new processes. Teams steward the 12 service indicators to maintain their quality-improvement focus.

Fed Ex has 43% of the domestic market; its nearest competitor has 26%.

"The winds and waves are always on the side of the ablest navigators."

Edward Gibson

IBM ROCHESTER, ROCHESTER, MN
INTERMEDIATE COMPUTER MANUFACTURING
1990 Baldrige Winner

IBM had this to report as to why the company adopted Total Quality Management:

Dramatic increase in global competition and a need for a culture change from a technology-driven process of delivering new products to a market-driven one prompted IBM's sharpened focus on TQM principles.

Six criteria guide the Strategic Quality Initiatives:

- Improved product and service requirements
- Enhanced product strategy
- Six sigma defect elimination (approximately three per million)
- Cycle-time reductions
- Improved education
- Increased employee involvement and ownership

Each senior manager "owns" one of the six factors and assumes responsibility for plans, implementations and monitoring progress. Hundreds of worldwide teams are in place. **Quality Goals** are in five-year plans and in annual operating plans. Targets are determined from benchmarking.

Quality-Improvement Plans

Each quality-improvement plan has an owner who may be either a manager or non-manager. Objectives are established, roles and responsibilities are clarified, inputs are determined and a measurement system is developed in advance of the project to capture data. Customers and suppliers meet regularly in planning meetings.

For example, more than 4,500 worldwide customers and business partners (suppliers) participated in advisory councils in the development of the AS/400 computer.

Each quality-improvement plan has an owner who may be either a manager or non-manager.

23

Guiding Principles

- Customer focus
- Total quality
- Global information systems
- Advisory councils
- Trials of prototypes
- 40 data sources analyzed to guide improvements
- Customers, employees, business partners all participate in solving the problems and making a better product and service

Training and Employee Development

- 5% of payroll is spent on training
- Communication skills and working in teams are the initial focus
- On-line management system helps employees plan their education and professional development
- Annual employee morale survey supplies IBM with worldwide input
- Recognition system supports TQM environment

Impact of TQM

- 30% improvement in productivity (1986-1989)
- 60% trim in manufacturing cycle
- 50% decrease in time for new product development
- Threefold increase in product reliability
- Increase from three to 12 months for product warranty
- Invested $30 million for processing information systems to focus on prevention instead of defection

Benchmarking

- Worldwide analysis of products and services to determine "best in the breed" in all industries

Goal in 1993

Hundredfold improvement and six sigma defect level by 1994. (Six sigma equals approximately three defects per million.)

"Innovative companies are especially adroit at continually responding to change of any sort in their environments."

Tom Peters

24

TQM PERFORMANCE RATING

How TQM Practices and Principles Can Improve Your Performance

Review the following list to see how your performance as a small-business owner, manager or supervisor will improve by putting the principles of TQM to work with the people in your area. Place one of the following numbers in front of each item to demonstrate your strength in your current TQM practices.

1   **Aware but not active**
2   **Aware but lacking in know-how in this area**
3   **Active with some applications**
4   **Leading in my department but not linking with peers or boss**
5   **Leading in my department and linking with peers and boss**

Your goal is to progress from 1 to 5 in each area. Find out what barriers exist for you and tackle the key issues that prevent your full success as a TQM manager or supervisor.

VISION, MISSION, GOALS

____   Align your understanding with that of your boss and your subordinates.

____   Keep employees informed about the company's achievements — market share, growth, new product development, competitor position.

____   Help employees link their daily efforts with the company's goals.

CUSTOMER SATISFACTION (INTERNAL AND EXTERNAL)

____ Survey and capture customer feedback to current products and services delivered by your people.

____ Communicate with customers to discover improvements and upgrades to products, services and processes.

____ Provide analysis of customer feedback and seek adjustments in current systems and service.

EMPLOYEE PARTICIPATION/TRAINING

____ Learn about each employee's strengths and weaknesses and what expectations each has for personal performance.

____ Set individual goals and objectives (aligned with the company) with each employee to maximize performance and set standards for excellence.

____ Empower employees to seek improvements to processes and systems around them.

____ Provide training in communications, team problem-solving, and TQM principles and tools.

TEAM SYNERGY/PROCESS IMPROVEMENTS

____ Establish a baseline of current productivity.

____ Set goals for improvements in systems and performance.

____ Create measurement systems that employees use to track progress.

____ Create cross-functional teams to troubleshoot improvements in work-process flows, operational systems and measurement with the goals of adding value for the customer and eliminating waste.

____ Establish rewards and incentives that recognize individual contributions as well as the team effort.

*C*HAPTER 3

TQM Implementation Overview

INTRODUCTION

Many attempts to implement Total Quality Management have failed largely because people perceive that "this is another fad program" or "this too shall pass." You may have heard or even used these expressions to describe changes in your company.

If TQM is to be successful in your company, it must become a part of the business. In fact, TQM is an approach to help manage the business by meeting the customer's needs.

The TQM Implementation Model provides a conceptual framework for you and your company to use as you develop your own continuous-improvement process. The components of the TQM Model represented here are found in all quality-improvement processes. Each company and department must work through these interrelated components; some are concurrent, others sequential. All these factors are critical to achieve TQM commitment and implementation.

> *"Quality is a habit, not an act."*
>
> *Aristotle*

Typically, companies enlist the support of a consultant to conduct a TQM Readiness Audit of both the organization and management as they currently function. An objective consultant's eye is generally considered to be more valid in conducting the audit. The viewpoints of top management, customers, suppliers and a vertical slice of employees from functions throughout the company are obtained.

The results of the audit provide a baseline assessment for management to review. Given the evidence from the initial assessment, management will focus on several areas where it wants improvements.

At this point, management must see the company — all of its systems, processes and outputs — as a whole. The company is a critical grouping of resources organized to serve the needs of customers with specialized requirements. Management can commit to a company-wide quality-improvement process or delegate improvement strategies to a problem-solving team.

Companies that embark on the road of continuous improvement through TQM make the following commitments:

1. The CEO and senior management lead the process through visionary leadership and provide enough resources for TQM to succeed.

2. A steering committee, composed of senior management and key players from throughout and outside of the company, receives ongoing TQM training in problem-solving and conflict resolution — as well as direction in leading a change process within an organization.

3. Preparation for implementing TQM or any change process (Chapter 8) must be finely tuned and integrated before it is launched. Time to assign roles, develop strategy, assemble resources and ready the environment to accept change are key tasks to accomplish at this point.

4. The principles of TQM — elimination of waste, error-free work and continuous improvement — are captured by focusing on

    - Customer Requirements (Chapter 4)
    - Measurement (Baselines and Benchmarks) (Chapter 11)
    - Existing Programs Aimed at Quality (Chapter 12)
    - Customer Service and Satisfaction (Chapter 13)

5. Training (Chapter 9) guides the entire process and never stops for the company's employees or suppliers if continuous improvement is the goal.

6. Evaluation (Chapter 14) provides an ongoing process for assessing the value and impact of quality on the performance of the company.

Exercise

Review the TQM Implementation Model on the next page to understand how all these components are united in continuous improvement. Think about how active you and your company are right now with parts of this model. Then, review the Five Steps of Commitment on page 31 and complete the exercise that invites you to create your vision of improving a process using the steps on page 32.

Exercise

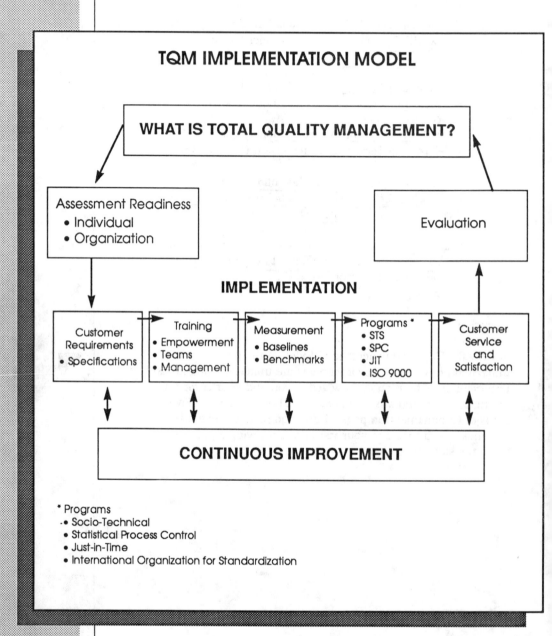

TQM IMPLEMENTATION MODEL

WHAT IS TOTAL QUALITY MANAGEMENT?

Assessment Readiness
- Individual
- Organization

Evaluation

IMPLEMENTATION

| Customer Requirements • Specifications | Training • Empowerment • Teams • Management | Measurement • Baselines • Benchmarks | Programs * • STS • SPC • JIT • ISO 9000 | Customer Service and Satisfaction |

CONTINUOUS IMPROVEMENT

* Programs
- Socio-Technical
- Statistical Process Control
- Just-in-Time
- International Organization for Standardization

TQM AS PROCESS IMPROVEMENT

As business strategies continue to evolve, it is clear that you will be required to improve performance and productivity while reducing costs. In the Japanese system the focus is on process improvement or *kaizen*. The idea is that much can be achieved by innovation, but competitive advantage is largely affected by continuous process improvement. To implement this practice, a commitment is necessary that includes a plan of action.

Five Steps of Commitment

Commitment means being the best you can be in your job, as well as continuously looking for opportunities to improve the work. Listed below is a five-step process designed to help you turn opportunities into on-the-job improvements.

1. **Awareness:**   Recognizing an opportunity to improve a process.

2. **Assessment:**   Identifying the gap between where you are and where you want to be.

3. **Preparation:**   Developing strategy, assembling resources, going through readiness steps.

4. **Action Plan:**   Establishing specific goals, timebound steps and measurements to implement an improvement.

5. **Evaluation:**   Reviewing how well you met the goals established in the action plan. Replanning as needed.

Eliminate the "But we've always done it that way" mind-set.

EXERCISE: IMPROVING A PROCESS

Awareness: List a current opportunity you have to improve a process.

_____

_____

Assessment: Where would you like to be? What is the desired situation?

_____

_____

Preparation: How ready are you to take action?

_____

_____

Action Plan: How and when will you get there?   Target Date:

1.   1.
2.   2.
3.   3.
4.   4.

Evaluation: How will you evaluate the results?

_____

_____

A FEW SUCCESS FACTORS TO CONSIDER ...

1. Are you committed to continuous improvement? Is your leadership?

2. Do you know your internal and external customers' requirements ?

3. Do you have opportunities for education and training to upgrade your skills?

4. Do you have a vision for the future?

5. Do you have clear direction for your job?

This manual will help you respond to these and other critical concerns that you may have along the road of continuous improvement.

HOW COMPONENTS IN THE TQM IMPLEMENTATION MODEL ARE LINKED

WHAT'S AHEAD

CUSTOMER REQUIREMENTS Chapter 4

Key questions:

- What are the internal/external customer requirements?
- How can a company certify suppliers against its own customer requirements?
- How do you plan to meet your customer requirements?

ASSESSMENT OF TQM READINESS Chapter 7

Key questions:

- How do you create an awareness of the opportunities for improvement?
- How do you identify the gap between the current work environment and a TQM environment?

PREPARING FOR IMPLEMENTATION Chapter 8

Key questions:

- What are the building blocks for TQM implementation?
- How can you identify and remove barriers to successful implementation?

TRAINING AND DEVELOPMENT Chapter 9

Key questions:

- What are the new skills employees and managers need to be successful in a TQM company?
- What are some of the best ways to train people in the new skills?

TOOLS FOR PROBLEM-SOLVING Chapter 10

Key questions:

- What is the basic problem-solving process?
- What are the key tools to enhance individual and group problem-solving?

MEASUREMENTS Chapter 11

Key questions:

- How can individual, departmental and company measurements track performance?
- What tools help to establish baselines, benchmarks and a customer-driven measurement process?

FOUR PROGRAMS Chapter 12

Key questions:

- What are tools and programs that help improve the day-to-day work process?
- How can you put these programs to work for you?

CUSTOMER SERVICE AND SATISFACTION Chapter 13

Key questions:

- How well did you meet your customers' requirements?
- How do you determine customer satisfaction?

EVALUATION/ OPTIONS FOR THE FUTURE Chapter 14

Key questions:

- How do you know what the score is — did you make TQM progress?
- Where do you go next?

CHAPTER 4

Customer Requirements

INTRODUCTION

Success in today's global marketplace mandates that customer requirements become the cornerstone upon which a company organizes its resources and dedicates its production. As companies pursue continuous-improvement efforts aimed at eliminating waste and reducing costs, the driving measurement of success will be the company's ability to satisfy customer requirements.

Companies need to stop being product-driven — where resources are aligned around the company's "technology" (what they invented; what they sell). They need to become market-driven — where the needs of customers of clearly defined market segments are the heart of every employee's job. When market needs drive business strategy, companies will partner with their suppliers in delivering high quality and "Best Cost" to their customers.

When companies commit to achieving "Best Cost" for their customers, they commit to doing those things that add value to the product or service; everything that is done that does not add value is considered to be waste. The cost of noncompliance (championed by Feigenbaum and Juran) really

> *"The customer can have any color car as long as it's black."*
>
> *Henry Ford*

37

makes the point that companies cannot afford NOT to meet customer requirements. The strength and success of business partnerships are dependent on understanding customer requirements.

Understanding customer requirements is a critical first step in the customer chain. Clarity up-front in the process means that the time is taken early on to learn about the customer and to understand the unique needs and objectives in buying a particular product or service.

Defining requirements clearly and identifying all the internal and external customers in the customer chain are the keys in detailing the process flow of work and establishing a definitive scope of service. Planning and agreement in the early stage prevents (or minimizes) rework later in the process. Perhaps more than any other single variable, meeting customer requirements guarantees customer satisfaction and a successful working relationship that serves all parties now and in the future.

WHAT IS A CUSTOMER?*

A Customer is the most important person ever in this office ... in person or by mail.

A Customer is not dependent on us ... we are dependent on him.

A Customer is not an interruption of our work ... he is the purpose of it. We are not doing a favor by serving him ... he is doing us a favor by giving us the opportunity to do so.

A Customer is not someone to argue or match wits with. Nobody ever won an argument with a Customer.

A Customer is a person who brings us his wants. It is our job to handle them profitably for him and for ourselves.

(A poster that is prominently displayed all around L.L. Bean, which serves customers 24 hours a day in its Freeport, Maine, home-office retail facility)

*Noted in Tom Peters' *A Passion for Excellence*, Random House (New York), 1985.

> *"Personal service has become a maddeningly rare commodity in the American marketplace."*
>
> **TIME Magazine**

Who Is the Customer?

In Japanese, the same word — *okyakusama* — means both "customer" and "honorable guest." Disney World has always thought of its customers as its "guests"; and many companies address their customers as being part of their "family." Customers in today's marketplace are looking for the special treatment that typically honors guests — and they are receiving it.

One definition explains that a customer is anybody who uses the output of your job; this description recognizes both internal and external customers. Another definition describes a customer as anybody who uses the products and services of a company; this one places a greater focus on the external customer.

The first definition also provides the entry for suppliers in the customer chain. Companies are beginning to develop their own customer requirements for suppliers. Some companies are even requiring that suppliers go through a vendor-certification process to guarantee that the supplier has the capability to perform at the level of excellence required by the company.

Customers have become more sophisticated consumers and are taking their role as "world-class shoppers" very seriously. The customer chain may include a number of suppliers and various internal customers, as well as the end user, client or the ultimate (external) customer — around which all others must understand that their work efforts are being directed.

Internal Customer

Frequently, the concept of the internal customer is one of the most difficult for companies to understand. Departments intent on fulfilling the needs of their external customers may overlook the needs of their own internal customers. When time is short, it is often the internal customer who gets shortchanged.

Companies that practice quality methods will create processes that link all the players in the customer chain — looking for "Best Cost" strategies that respond to customer requirements at every step. Responsiveness to people is an inherent value in quality companies; and a request from a colleague at work becomes primary in delivering the best service to the external customer.

Work is organized to make it more efficient. How responsive individuals within an organization are to one another will be reflected in how external customers are treated as well.

External Customer (the Ultimate Customer)

Companies that differentiate market segments and begin to fine-tune their niche markets are the companies that will become most responsive to their customers. "Getting close to the customer" is a requirement for total-quality companies. Customers are setting the pace and pushing innovation and product adaptation through unprecedented product-development cycle times.

In order to serve their customers better, companies have sought improvement in their own methods and performance. Examples include such things as Just-in-Time (JIT) manufacturing and cultural-diversity programs. Total-quality companies are focused on improving their productivity and passing on savings to their customers.

Suppliers as Partners

New value is being assigned to relationships with suppliers in serving customers. TQM has provided the opportunity for an expanded awareness of a supplier's role and impact on the results of a company in delivering its products and services to its ultimate customer. Companies are embracing suppliers as full partners in planning, designing, providing and evaluating their services and products for customers.

In order for a company to achieve its best performance, suppliers must be held to the same standards of excellence as the company. Vendor-certification processes establish requirements for suppliers that qualify them to provide products and services for the company, under the same competitive conditions for high quality and excellence in which the company must operate.

Ford Motor Co.'s famous Q101 program provides suppliers with a process through which they receive a treasured "Q1" Rating. Only the very best suppliers receive the even more prized "TQE" (Total Quality Excellence) Rating — and only after they have held the "Q1" Rating for several consecutive years.

Other companies such as Corning and General Motors have adopted similar supplier-assessment programs to strengthen the quality of their suppliers to meet their requirements. Companies are taking their supplier partnerships very seriously and are passing along quality and savings to the end customer.

As you review the Vendor Certification Program and evaluate your own company based on GM's criteria for suppliers, note the possible actions you, your department or your company might take now to improve in a specific area. While the criteria are based on GM's customer requirements for its suppliers, the items will provide you with ideas about your own customer requirements.

The continuous pursuit of EXCELLENCE.

41

A SAMPLE VENDOR CERTIFICATION PROGRAM: CRITERIA FOR ASSESSMENT

The following criteria will provide you with an example of how suppliers might be evaluated in the process of becoming a certified supplier. Each company must develop its own assessment process and criteria for evaluating its suppliers.

Certification programs provide an opportunity for a company to define its requirements related to the performance of suppliers. The criteria are applied uniformly throughout all divisions within the company to provide a clearly identified group of high-quality suppliers. Certification programs typically share common goals such as:

- Increased quality
- Reduced cost
- Continuous improvement
- Qualifying "top" performing suppliers and eliminating those that do not meet customer requirements

A certification process usually has several parts including:

1. **Supplier Identification** — Companies apply initial screening mechanisms to determine a supplier's potential for meeting the company's vendor requirements and cost reductions in the future.

2. **Pre-Assessment Preparation** — After a supplier is selected for assessment, an assessment team is appointed to perform activities such as:

   - Collect and analyze the supplier's historical, corporate data
   - Explain evaluation criteria (customer requirements) to the supplier
   - Provide supplier with an assessment packet with things such as a letter from the company conducting the certification, the company's (customer) requirements and the supplier questionnaire with all the criteria itemized

Certification programs provide an opportunity for a company to define its requirements related to the performance of suppliers.

The pre-assessment allows a supplier to conduct its own evaluation process to see how it would rate itself against the certifying company's specific criteria. A supplier may postpone the formal certification process until it is in better compliance with customer requirements. To improve itself, a supplier may ask the company granting the certification for help. Some companies have formal training programs for suppliers to take to become certified suppliers of the company.

Win
Win

3. **On-Site Assessment** — An assessment team from the company will visit suppliers after they have gone through a preparation phase that makes them feel ready to proceed with the certification process. The on-site assessment includes interviews with various personnel of the supplier, examination of its procedures, record-keeping and results. The assessment team must reach consensus on how to rate the supplier and complete a final report. (Refer to sample "Vendor Performance Rating" to review a possible list of evaluation criteria.)

4. **Post-Assessment** — After a supplier has gone through the formal certification process, several outcomes are possible:

- All ratings are compiled and placed in the company's supplier database so anyone in the company now has access to performance information on that supplier.

- Suppliers may be requested to present a plan for corrective action to address areas of deficiency and begin a process to improve in particular areas and/or achieve certification.

QUALITY is everyone's job.

43

- A new assessment may be planned because of
  - the company's desire to have a long-term relationship with the supplier
  - the supplier's commitment to pursue its own improvement and compliance with customer requirements
  - new data from the supplier since its initial assessment to warrant a review

- The company may direct suppliers toward various supplier-development activities — both for suppliers who achieved certification and for those who did not.

VENDOR PERFORMANCE RATING

Each company must establish its own customer requirements around which it designs criteria for certification. Suppliers are assessed and rated on those criteria. The following is a sample outline of assessment criteria modeled after GM's Supplier Assessment Process. Pretend your operation is applying for supplier certification and see how you would rate your self. The Readiness Questionnaire can be completed by managers and team members from different departments to provide the organization with a cross-functional view of supplier/vendor performance. Note what action you, your department or your company could take to improve in specific areas. This exercise will demonstrate how customer requirements will drive quality along the entire customer chain.

Rating Scale

5 Demonstrates highest capability; quality process of its own in place; continuous-improvement process in place

4 Effective planning and implementation demonstrated; minor improvements in systems, operations and/or commitment can result in demonstrated performance improvements

3 Improvements expected in system or implementation; corrective action required

2 Major improvements expected; commitment to improve demonstrated and documented

1 Critical deficiencies observed; lack of commitment to improve

VENDOR PERFORMANCE RATING — READINESS QUESTIONNAIRE

In responding to each of the sample questions, (1) identify the system or process in place to achieve each item under question and (2) identify the efforts your company uses to ensure that the system or process can be improved based on feedback from your continuous-improvement process. Note actions you, your department or your company can take to improve specific areas.

SAMPLE QUESTIONS

MANAGEMENT

1. Describe organizational structure and discuss how effective it is in supporting the output of the company.

2. How does your company communicate your operating philosophy and business-control systems throughout the company?

3. Do you have a system for soliciting employee ideas and keeping employees informed about the company?

4. Does your company review its business plan annually with its employees?

EFFECTIVE HUMAN RESOURCE MANAGEMENT

1. Does the company have a training-and-development program that prepares employees with the skills they need?

2. How does the company communicate job expectations to employees and how does it provide feedback on performance?

EFFECTIVE HUMAN RESOURCE MANAGEMENT (continued)

3. How does your company evaluate job satisfaction of employees?

4. Does the company reflect "pride of place" in its organization and maintenance of its physical plant?

5. What provisions are made to assure employee health and safety?

QUALITY OF SUBCONTRACTORS

1. Does the selection process align with the same quality standards that the company expects of itself?

2. Does the company evaluate the performance of subcontractors and help them improve?

RESPONSIVENESS TO NEEDS

How does the company as a supplier ensure that you are meeting the needs of our company?

QUALITY

1. Does your quality plan describe specific activities at every level of the organization that are focused on improving our product and service?

2. Do your quality procedures provide sufficient guidance to carry out the quality plan?

QUALITY CONTROL

1. Does your statistical process control (SPC) address out-of-control or unstable processes?

2. Are instructions for in-process and final inspections/tests sufficient to ensure that quality standards are met?

3. Does your documentation for calibration of measurement devices include actions to be taken when a device does not meet the standard?

4. Does your procedure for material identification include actions for ensuring traceability of all finished material and segregation of nonconforming material?

QUALITY CONTROL (continued)

5. Does your drawing and specification-control procedure ensure that only up-to-date versions are used?

6. Do your internal auditors have the records necessary to evaluate the quality of your operations?

CORRECTIVE ACTION IN RESPONSE TO NONCONFORMANCE

1. Who within your company is responsible for notifying us that you may have received nonconforming materials?

2. Does your procedure for problem resolution include identification of root causes and verification of corrective action?

CONTROL OF SUBCONTRACTORS

1. Do you have a system for assessing, selecting and developing a source/subcontractor base to ensure that your company's and our expectations are met?

2. Does your system for reviewing purchased materials and services ensure requirements are met?

COST

1. Can you document how you determine the basis for labor, material and overhead rates?

2. How do you document the efficiency of labor hours and the use of materials?

3. When you review actual costs monthly, what is your system for taking action to reduce unnecessary costs?

COST REDUCTION

1. How do you document improvements in your operation that lead to cost reductions?

2. Do you have historical data to show that you have stayed within budgeted costs?

3. What documentation can you provide to show detailed evaluation of piece prices?

4. How does your company use historical data for cost estimates?

DELIVERY

1. How much lead time do you need to increase production by 10%?

2. Does your scheduling system include at least weekly communication with your customer?

3. How do you communicate information to the appropriate personnel when your schedule is not met?

4. What is your system for coordination between production and shipping?

5. How do you ensure that your inventory on hand is appropriate?

6. How do you ensure that premium shipments are kept to a minimum?

SHIPMENT NOTIFICATION TO CUSTOMER

What level of your company's management is responsible for notifying a customer that a shipment might be delayed?

PACKAGING AND SHIPPING

1. Does your company have documentation to show that part-count audits are performed on a random basis by someone other than the packer?

2. How does your labeling system ensure that each package is labeled correctly?

3. How is your material-handling system designed to reduce damage to materials?

4. Is your shipping and receiving area sufficient to handle your activities?

TECHNOLOGY

1. How do you ensure input from the relevant disciplines and users in designing your products?

2. Does your company have a plan to extend the use of computer-aided design?

3. How do you use data from performance testing of your product?

TECHNOLOGY (continued)

4.   How do you ensure the input from the relevant disciplines and users are involved in prototype development?

5.   How do you document the results and applications of your research and development projects?

MANUFACTURING CAPABILITIES

1.   How do you evaluate the effectiveness of your production activities based on equipment and human-performance data?

2.   Do you have data to show the effectiveness of your preventive-maintenance scheduling?

3.   Does your tooling management system allow you to meet schedule and product requirements?

INCREASING CUSTOMER INTERFACE OPPORTUNITIES

There are many ways to increase the number of opportunities for productive interface with customers. The following are some examples of successful ways through which companies strengthen client relationships:

- Users' conferences

- Customer product-design teams

- Problem-solving customer groups

- Customer-satisfaction surveys (Chapter 11)

- Pilot programs to market-test new products

- Cross-training in jobs that may serve as linchpins between the company and the client

Your early efforts to set the stage for developing productive relationships with efficient and clear communication may serve you better than anything else in working with your customers. You will want to use the checklist on the next page in preparation for customer interface.

Once you have established a relationship of mutual trust and respect, you will be in a solid position from which to work through difficulties that may arise. Your appreciation of one another's business cycles, technologies and human-resource needs provides rich understanding for working together.

> *"The best way to understand your customer is to become your customer and walk a mile in his shoes."*
>
> **Ian D. Littman**

53

CHECKLIST FOR MEETING CUSTOMER REQUIREMENTS

_____ Frequent communication with customer representatives at many levels throughout the customer's company

    _____ Face-to-face meetings   _____ Telephone
    _____ Questionnaires/surveys   _____ Other
    _____ Letters of praise/complaint

_____ Time allocated to develop a relationship with the customer in which mutual trust and respect evolve from a thorough understanding of one another's industry, business, driving forces and critical factors

_____ Standard information scan for meeting customer requirements such as detailed product/service specifications, minimum delivery time, warranty required and employees on point for various project phases

_____ Inclusion of suppliers and subcontractors in assessing a Request for Bid (RFB) including client interface

_____ Sufficient time allocated during the planning stage of a project to achieve a thorough understanding of customer requirements, scope of service, division of responsibilities, and desired working style and reporting system

_____ Tracking systems for monitoring success at meeting customer requirements

_____ Corrective-action process in place for improving in areas where customer requirements were not met

_____ Certification process and training programs to educate, orient and evaluate employees, customers and suppliers to meet customer requirements

_____ Customer surveys to assess their satisfaction and solicit their input for desired improvements or innovations

_____ Employee exchange assignments for deepening understanding of customer-supplier requirements and experience

_____ Users' conference

_____ Expanded opportunities for customer interface

    _____ Problem-solving teams
    _____ Benchmarking teams
    _____ Product-design teams
    _____ Pilot program to test market new product
    _____ Other: _____
                _____
                _____
                _____
                _____

```
  1    2    3    4    5    6    7    8    9    10
```

Traditional   **TQM**
Structure   **Focus**

Place an "X" where you feel your company currently fits.

*C*HAPTER 5

Origin of Modern Quality
Principles and Practices

INTRODUCTION

Has any other nation achieved any greater economic
turnaround during this century than Japan? Actually, it has
taken only a few short decades since World War II for the U.S.
consumer to transform an upturned nose at the label "Made in
Japan" as indicative of inferior quality to the "thumbs-up" sign
recognizing excellence in Japanese quality and technology.
Have you ever wondered how the Japanese really did it?

As you review the events that supported post-war American
market dominance with mass production and then the
emergence of Japan as an economic superpower, note how
practicing the principles of Total Quality Management shaped
U.S. and Japanese technological and economic leadership.
You will appreciate the increased importance of "getting close
to your customers" to meet their requirements in order to
maintain good clients and deliver quality goods and services.

TQM provides a meeting of Eastern and Western philosophy
and extracts precision and know-how from both parts of the
globe. No single culture has all the answers. The advancement
of TQM demonstrates the power of a united effort. While it is
true the competitor "down the street" may now be from

halfway around the world, the common thread among successful companies of the future will be their commitment to quality and continuous improvement. Customers will continue to demand better quality, and suppliers will partner with companies to meet customer requirements.

TQM AND THE ECONOMIC RECOVERY OF POST-WAR JAPAN

During its post-war assessment of Japanese manufacturing, the Americans had concluded that Japanese engineering wasn't so bad but that Japanese management needed an overhaul. Karou Ishikawa, one of the quality leaders, and other Japanese working with him thought that the American statistical methods and procedures had value but that they would have to adapt American management theories to reflect Japanese norms and culture.

The Japanese have contributed much from their culture to the gifts of statistical methods brought to them by Deming and the strategy of managing for quality brought to them by Juran. William Ouchi's *Theory Z* (1981) details how the Japanese infused their own roots in developing Japanese management systems. Many of the most fundamental principles of TQM come from Japanese culture. Trust, long-term commitment, collaboration, emulation, reciprocity, subtlety and the discipline of incremental and continuous improvement are but a few of the foundation blocks in TQM that mirror Japanese culture.

Western management theories, such as Douglas McGregor's Theory Y, recognize the creativity and ingenuity of workers and encourage the development of work environments that stimulate and reward such individual contributions. It was the Japanese, however, who first understood that the contributions had to come from all workers at all levels and that the rewards had to be shared among all the contributors in the organization.

Refer to the chart "Quality — the Key to Japan's Economic Recovery" on page 61, which shows the thinking that guided top management in Japan from 1950 onward. The Japanese strategy, developed with them by Deming and Juran, was to deliver higher quality at a lower price. Deming predicted Japan's success in the following quote:

"The year 1950 was the beginning of a new Japan in quality. I predicted in 1950 that Japanese products would within five years invade the markets of the world, and that the standard of living in Japan would in time rise to equality with the world's most prosperous countries.

The basis for my confidence in this prediction was

    (1) observations on the Japanese workforce;
    (2) knowledge and devotion to their jobs by Japanese management;
    (3) faith that Japanese management would accept and carry out their responsibilities;
    (4) expansion of education by JUSE [Japanese Union of Scientists and Engineers]."

Dr. W. Edwards Deming
Out of the Crisis
MIT, 2nd ed., 1986

THE EMERGENCE OF JAPAN AS AN ECONOMIC SUPERPOWER

During World War II, American companies answered government pleas by focusing on mass production. Never before had any nation in the history of the world called their production forces into such incessant and dedicated production. Quantity and quality were synonymous with "getting the job done right the first time and on schedule."

U.S. military operations required "fail safe" technology for all strategic vessels and weaponry, as well as highly sophisticated navigation and communications equipment. The development and application of the most advanced technology the world had ever seen was placed under the most stringent quality research and production standards. The demand for continuous production coupled with the military's need for guaranteed precision and accuracy began the quality movement.

> *QUANTITY and QUALITY -*
>
> *getting the job done right the first time and on schedule.*

At the end of World War II, the United States controlled a third of the world economy and made half of the manufactured goods sold anywhere in the world. American industry responded to fueling a peacetime economy through mass production. Quantity was the goal, not response to "specialty" markets requiring distinct manufacturing processes. Industry believed it could not slow down to accommodate the few when there were so many others ready to buy the standard. The world was on a consumer binge, and America just kept turning out product.

Top-level corporate executives saw no advantage in pursuing quality over quantity. American management saw Quality Control as the purview of engineering, for which manufacturing was responsible. The concept of "Acceptable Quality Levels" (AQL), as expressed in defects per hundred, became the standard for American manufacturing. For U.S. firms, quality was an inspection issue. Higher quality standards would mean more inspection and higher cost. Management thus concluded that higher quality would always mean higher costs.

The Japanese have proven this conclusion incorrect. They trained everyone to analyze their jobs and to seek opportunities for ways to improve how their work was done. They kept their procedures flexible and took pride in the challenge of perfecting a process by incremental improvements. They began to define quality as a "constant reduction in variability." The Japanese raised their goals steadily and continued to apply the formula they had been using since 1950.

The Japanese ability to produce high-quality, low-cost goods became stronger and stronger. Deming's statistical methods to trim variations to a hairline, Juran's management concepts combined with Ishikawa's Quality Circles, and Taguchi's robusting and Loss Function to stop deviance at its source all provided Japanese manufacturers with powerful and competitive tools.

Japan had been analyzing various U.S. industries since the war and was eager to take on the challenge of direct competition with U.S. companies. Japanese companies offered superior reliability and lower cost than American manufacturers. It was

At the end of World War II, the United States controlled a third of the world economy.

60

a competitive strategy few could refute in the early 1970s — or the early 1990s.

Japan's strategy was to attack at the low end of the market and build credibility from there. By entering markets at the low end, many Japanese companies generated the volume they needed in order to go after the high-price end of the market later. When the Japanese went after the higher end of a market, they did so with the same strategy. They offered a superior product at a lower cost than their U.S. competitors.

A long list of U.S. industries have fallen prey to this strategy. From machine tools to automobiles, from cameras to diesel engines, from steel to VCRs, from electronics to advanced computer technology — Japan has been reclaiming its position in the world through a relentless commitment to quality. Japan has successfully chipped away at American market dominance. The advent of Japanese economic muscle in the world might have been avoided had the United States chosen the same commitment to higher quality, reduced cost and TQM work environments as Japan did after World War II.

The advent of Japanese economic muscle in the world might have been avoided had the United States chosen the same commitment to higher quality, reduced cost and TQM work environments.

TOTAL QUALITY MANAGEMENT: IMPACT

Quality — the Key to Japan's Economic Recovery

The following chain reaction was on the blackboard of every top management meeting in Japan from early 1950 onward (Deming).

Improve Quality	Costs Decrease	Produc-tivity Improves	Capture the Market	Stay in Business	Provide Jobs and More Jobs

— Less rework

— Fewer mistakes

— Fewer delays

— Better use of machine time and materials

— Better quality

— Lower price

CHAPTER 6

The Quality Gurus

INTRODUCTION

Deming. Juran. Feigenbaum. Crosby. Ishikawa. Taguchi. These are some of the prominent pioneers in the quality movement. Their tenacity to perfect a process of concurrent and integrated systems and to gain better control of variance within those processes and systems has created an irreversible impact on the way work is done. To succeed in the marketplace, companies must fully embrace the customer-driven concepts of TQM by optimizing resources to deliver the highest-quality product at the lowest cost.

As you review the core concepts of these foundation thinkers, notice their similarities and the way they build upon one another. It is at once both very American and very Japanese "to be the best" at something. It is no wonder the quality movement has spurred what some are calling the "quality revolution." The combination of the American pioneer spirit to discover and invent and the Japanese drive to perfect the most successful improvements of new technologies are important themes in the quality movement.

The quality gurus set the baseline for achieving excellence in producing quality. Those who have been eager to follow in

> *"No one knows what it is that he can do until he tries."*
>
> **Publilius Syrus**

QUALITY

QUALITY

QUALITY!

their footsteps are now setting new baselines against which others benchmark. The adventurous, the committed, the ingenious, the tenacious — those are the ones who shout, "Quality at Any Cost," "Quality First" and "Quality Is Job 1."

The legacy is a rich one. The quality gurus prompted what is fast becoming the norm for how companies operate today and in the future. There is no slipping back along the quality curve; customers won't tolerate it. Quality is a way of life for the companies who are capturing loyal customers. Take a look at some of the benefits of TQM and then meet the people who started the movement.

Benefits for Companies That Practice TQM ... (Just a Few)

- Reduced costs in bringing high-quality product to market
- Sustained profit and market growth
- Higher success rate with new product introduction
- Greater retention of customers and attraction of new ones
- Better design, decreased cycle times, longer "shelf-life"
- Supplier partnerships in meeting customer requirements
- Improved morale and increased employee participation
- Stronger employee loyalty from team productivity and reward

W. EDWARDS DEMING

W. Edwards Deming (1900-   ), who resides in Washington, D.C., ranks with General Douglas MacArthur as one of the most famous Americans in Japan. His contribution to post-war Japan has been cited as a pivotal factor in the rebuilding of its economy. Deming provided both a philosophy and a methodology in applying statistical methods to achieve higher quality and productivity in manufacturing and management.

In the 1950s Deming promised Japan that the methods he taught would not only help it rebuild its industries at home after the war but would enable it to compete in world markets in the future. He told Japan it would compete through continuous improvement and the elimination of waste. Higher-quality products would be produced at lower cost.

Japan had just been devastated by the war and was occupied by the Allied Forces. With few natural resources, the Japanese wisely calculated the need to develop their technological intelligence. Deming offered the Japanese hope for their stake in the future. He believed their commitment to quality would help them advance, and so did they.

Walter Shewhart and his colleagues at Bell Labs in the 1930s provided the research foundation for the development of Statistical Process Control (SPC). Shewhart combined the principles of quality control with statistics and probabilities to develop Statistical Quality Control.

Shewhart referred Deming to Homer Sarasohn, a Bell colleague, to teach statistical methods in Japan. Sarasohn and Deming trained the Japanese to produce communications equipment that would accommodate the needs of the occupation forces to inform and educate the nation of its progress during rebuilding. Further, Sarasohn and Deming used the communications industry as an example of how the Japanese economy could be revived.

Deming was tenacious about his assignment and so were the Japanese. Years later, Deming recalls his first class in Japan: "I've never had better students. I'd describe them as the top 5% of all classes I've ever taught."

Deming's contribution to post-war Japan has been cited as a pivotal factor in the rebuilding of its economy.

It was Shewhart's Cycle of Plan, Do, Check and Act (PDCA) that became the Deming Cycle of Plan, Do, Study and Act (PDSA) in Japan and provided the logic behind SPC methods. Joseph Juran, also with Bell, was invited by Shewhart to Japan in 1954, after the publication of *Quality Control Handbook* (1951).

Companies that have worked with Deming explain he will probe all the difficult issues in the organization. He is a holistic thinker and doer and will challenge others to work in that framework. Deming understands that in order to change behavior, an organization will have to rethink its attitudes, beliefs and values. "We've always done it this way" is a challenge for all companies that want to remain competitive.

Today, Japan's most coveted prize recognizing industrial quality is the Deming Award. (Only one American company has won this award: Florida Power and Light in 1989.) In 1960, Deming received The Second Order Medal of the Sacred Treasurer, the highest award Japan can bestow on a foreigner. Deming still gives guest lectures and teaches his four-day seminar in quality.

Deming's Challenge for Management

Deming believes quality is 85% the responsibility of management and 15% the responsibility of employees. Quality Circles, developed in Japan in the late 1950s and early 1960s (based on Western management theories such as Douglas McGregor's Theory Y), addressed only the 15% that belonged to the employees. Deming developed his 14 Points as a "Charter for Management" to seek management's commitment to quality.

The three key ingredients of Deming's 14 Points are:

- Constancy of purpose
- Continual improvement
- Profound knowledge

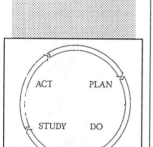

ACT   PLAN

STUDY   DO

W. Edwards Deming

The 14 Points are described in detail in this manual where Deming's thoughts on constancy of purpose and continual improvement are represented. Profound knowledge is not one of the 14 Points, but, in fact, is an orientation management needs to embrace when leading a total quality process.

Deming's concept of **profound knowledge** sets him apart from the other quality gurus. Profound knowledge exemplifies Deming as a philosopher. It demonstrates the core beliefs and values about learning that have guided Japan's economic recovery and rise to world status. Deming's philosophy and methods are only now gaining widespread U.S. recognition for their impact on quality and productivity in U.S. companies.

Profound knowledge, according to Deming, comprises four broad categories:

- Appreciation for a system
- Theory of variation
- Theory of knowledge
- Psychology

Deming teaches that these components of knowledge are inseparable. To learn anything, one must commit to the whole.

Appreciation for the system is a starting point. Deming explains when every part of a system is working in support of another part, "optimization" occurs. To achieve optimization, Deming says all internal competition must be eliminated. Numerical ratings and rankings need to be eliminated in assessing and conveying feedback to individuals about their performance.

Deming makes two points about **variation.** First, errors and inconsistencies will always exist, and people apply the "wrong" corrective action when something goes wrong.

Many dollars are wasted as organizations try to understand what has caused a problem. Deming recommends applying the Shewhart/Deming Cycle to analyze a problem and to use Shewhart's Control Chart to track activity. As an event occurs, it is plotted at the given juncture on the X and Y axis, each representing a variable such as time and date.

Appreciation for a system, theory of variation, theory of knowledge and psychology are the four inseparable components of knowledge — they are profound knowledge.

"American
companies failed to
notice the trends.
They adhered to the
belief that Japanese
competition was
primarily price
competition rather
than quality
competition."

J.M. Juran

Deming views **knowledge** as a prediction that "comes true."
He believes that knowledge comes from theory and that
without theory, there is no learning. Without a theory of
knowledge that underlines experience, Deming states that an
organization cannot learn from its own experience or from that
of another company. An organization cannot "copy" another
company's success in total quality improvement or formulate a
"Total Quality Plan"; it is a process that each company must
develop on its own.

Psychology, according to Deming, is the most powerful
component of the three elements of profound knowledge. He
believes people want to learn and create. Unintentionally,
management frequently works against developing its
employees because ratings and rankings of employees rob
them of their internal motivation.

Train the people to measure "things," says Deming, and they
will keep pushing their own standards higher to "beat"
themselves. Organizations need to recognize that people learn
at different rates and in different ways. Training methods and
approaches need to increase learning for individuals and for
the organization itself.

Deming is both a philosopher and a pragmatist in his approach
to quality. He has provided both inspiration and discipline for
the human spirit. His life has been dedicated to enhancing
productivity and the quality of work life for organizations and
individuals. The application of profound knowledge in the
practice of TQM has made customers and suppliers central in
the goals of business.

Deming believes quality is a moving target because our needs
and expectations continuously change. Deming sees
"transformational" experiences in the workplace and in
individual lives — discipline and discovery over time — as
primary factors in measuring quality improvement in processes,
services and products.

Deming believes the inherent value of quality is in its pursuit.
How effective managers and supervisors are in aligning and
motivating their people to contribute their collective efforts to
achieve a common goal is quality's real challenge. The

common goal, ultimately, is customer satisfaction and business excellence.

The Shewhart/Deming Cycle: PDSA (PDCA) Cycle

Total quality and its commitment to continuous improvement require that work and processes be thought of in a circular system — not as a linear path of beginning, middle and end.

An entire process is analyzed and an aspect of the total process is isolated for improvement. Then, a plan is developed to achieve an improvement. Once the plan is clear, it is enacted. The results of enacting the plan are recorded, studied and assessed. Then, action is taken to incorporate the improvement into the process because it achieves the desired impact, to rework the change until it meets the mark or to reject the idea and create a new one.

In total quality, consensus determines whether a change in the process will take place. This means that all parties are satisfied at the moment with the outcome and that the improvement is recognized as a reduction in cost, cycle time or variance. In total quality, the next step is to attack another issue in the process and to repeat the cycle.

It is important to understand that the PDSA is a process cycle. Because frequently many people from various departments are involved and may experience a "breakthrough," a cycle can be thought of as a project. It is significant to maintain the perspective of the experience as a cycle, not as a one-time-only "project." Projects are completed steps in the continuous process of quality management.

Walter Shewhart conceived a cycle of Plan, Do, Check and Act (PDCA). Deming modified it to Plan, Do, Study and Act (PDSA) in 1990. This is called the Deming Cycle in Japan, and either the Shewhart or Deming Cycle in the United States.

Total quality and its commitment to continuous improvement require that work and processes be thought of in a circular system.

69

The Shewhart/Deming Cycle: Plan, Do, Study and Act

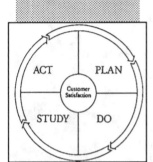

PLAN   Process improvements can be achieved at any level of organization within a company. Focusing on customer requirements and including input from upstream and downstream suppliers, internal customers and distributors will deliver the best results. Managers, supervisors and employees must troubleshoot the system and plan improvements together.

The Japanese spend considerably more time in the planning phase than their American counterparts. The pressure on managers in U.S. companies is to move quickly through planning to production. Frequently, this results in excessive time and money in rework.

DO   Once there is an initiative for improvement, it is acted out in a small-scale test. The Deming Cycle is a statistical device and allows employees to record variation and focus on incremental improvements. A manageable scope is identified, observations are recorded. The tools used to record observations are Flow Chart, Cause and Effect Diagram (Ishikawa Fishbone Diagram), Pareto Chart, Trend Chart, Histogram, Scatter Diagram and Control Chart. (See "The Seven Basic Tools" and the charts, pages 114 and 115.)

STUDY   All the results from the test are examined and discussed. The impact of elements of the test is related to all other aspects of the whole. Thorough analysis requires a clear understanding of these interrelationships.

ACT   Based on the aims of the test that were determined up front during planning, some decision is made to either adopt, adjust or abandon the plan. At this point, employees are back at the top of the cycle, ready to follow along the path of continuous improvement.

70

Case Study: The New Age Electronics Co. — the Shewhart/Deming Cycle

Now that you have been introduced to the Shewhart/Deming Cycle, review the following situation. Answer the questions to gain insight about how you can use the Shewhart/Deming Cycle as a tool in your department to increase quality and customer satisfaction.

Case Problem

Sales were down for the past three quarters for the New Age Electronics Co. Last year, Bill Raemore, the president of the company, launched a new program for sales representatives to become more knowledgeable about product design and capabilities. Mr. Raemore believes the way to increase sales is to put the sales reps in a better position to describe the product and its benefits. Each sales rep received three weeks of product training last year. The New Age Electronics Co., after 25 years of delivering reputable electronics components (not "stellar" but well-liked and appreciated for the "value" they provided), made history seven years ago when its patent for a new electronic connector turned heads in the industry. In fact, the company spends most of its resources now promoting that technological plum. The marketing budget for that product has grown enormously over the past two years: the brochures are glossier, the distribution is greater.

Raemore became president at the time the connector was introduced, and he is the chief national spokesperson for the product. He believes that the product will carry the company into the next century. Still, for all the increased investment of time and money, the results aren't there. There are rumors in the company that the product is becoming obsolete. A foreign competitor, who opened regional sales offices in the United States a year and a half ago, is just beginning to take off.

C A S E   S T U D Y

71

Raemore believes the drop in sales reflects the downturn in the economy. He expects great things as soon as some of the economic indicators improve. He is not threatened by the entrance of the foreign competitor because 87% of New Age's business is domestic. New Age is fully established and positioned with an entrenched U.S. distribution network that looks favorably upon the company.

Raemore has asked you, as the national sales manager, to look into this problem and to make recommendations about next year's budget expenditures for marketing the connector.

The New Age Electronics Co. ...

Case Questions

1. How do you define the problem?

2. Who else needs to be included?

3. What possible reasons might exist for a lack of market response?

4. What role should Mr. Raemore play in the analysis of this problem? What should your role be as the national sales manager?

5. Who is missing from the case problem?

6. Using the Shewhart/Deming Cycle, can you develop a strategy for assessing the situation and making some recommendations?

   Hint: Take advantage both of what has been said as well as what has been omitted in assessing the situation. Review the descriptions of steps in the Shewhart/Deming Cycle:

   Plan ——— Do ——— Study ——— Act

Case Analysis

PLAN — In troubleshooting what is happening with the New Age Electronics Co., you first need to think through what your role is as national sales manager in the assignment. Will you serve as a program manager and pull others together to go after some "answers" to Raemore's questions? Will you embrace the situation as your own? You will also need to think about Mr. Raemore's role: What does he need to experience in order to be part of the solution? Do you think he may be part of the problem? Why? How and when can you best engage him for the most productive results? Have you thought of the "missing" piece yet? If you said "The customer!" — you are already out in front of Raemore. Pull some people together to brainstorm a process for evaluating the problem and then begin to "Do." Demonstrate how the Shewhart/Deming Cycle works so people can become comfortable using it.

DO — Think through some of the "people" pieces: Who's who and what is his or her vested interest? Who has been left out and how can you include that person now in analyzing and troubleshooting the problem? Begin the steps of your analysis plan. Here are a few key suggestions:

1. Appoint a special Problem-Solving Team to troubleshoot the decrease in sales related to the connector. Seek diverse group membership from product design, production, sales, marketing, distribution, and customer service. Reach out to include suppliers and get the group to make a decision about when to involve the customer. Communication style and existing channels are very important considerations. Be thorough and invent some new ones.

C A S E   A N A L Y S I S

2. Brainstorm, survey and interview key stakeholders to obtain their input. Provide a quantitative assessment and distribution of opinion and facts and a narrative that identifies and contrasts diverse viewpoints and factors of influence. (Your group members may decide they would like training in problem-solving or consensus-building skills; or perhaps, they need training on how to use the tools for measurement.)

STUDY — Once you achieve a rich "core dump" of data, experience and reflections, focus the process on variables that have significant impact on the situation.

1. Develop a plan to assemble quantitative and qualitative data regarding the connector and demonstrating such factors as sales volume and fluctuations; customer satisfaction/dissatisfaction; unmet needs; wastes in production; breakdowns in distribution and service; information about the competition; return on investment (ROI) for marketing expenditures related to margins on product sold. By now, you should have achieved input from people in various positions throughout the company, the supplier base and the customers — especially the three major clients who recently left.

2. Plan and prepare the most effective method to inform the president of the results of your findings — including a synopsis of the Plan, Do and Study steps — as well as the interpretations of the team. The interpretations spell out the interrelationships of the variables as you have observed, collected and studied them.

ACT — After the results of the work of the Problem-Solving Team have been clearly presented to the president, the president can direct the group to adopt its recommendations, adjust them or abandon them — at which point the group is back at the top of the cycle and can begin again. As a team goes through the Shewhart/Deming cycle, the members learn new skills to define, assess, analyze and resolve problems. This method supports continuous improvement and engages a broad spectrum of players in the process.

Some Final Thoughts on Interpreting This Case Problem...

Some obvious problems contained within the case problem include:

1. The New Age Electronics Co. was product-driven. The company typifies the Product-Push side of the equation to the neglect of the Market-Pull side. This is a hard lesson for some companies to learn — especially those that have risen based on their technology.

2. In the case, the "star" product had become a "cash cow" and was on its way to becoming a "dog." This explains why more marketing dollars for glossier brochures and marketing distribution only created more drain and actually decreased ROI.

3. The president appears to be part of the problem. He is protective of the fading "star." Raemore is obviously misguided in thinking that this product will carry the company into the next century. He appears oblivious to the globalization of the economy, in which the foreign competitor down the street is nipping at the heels of the company's domestic market, while Raemore does nothing to address new markets nor shows concern that the company depends on the domestic market for 87% of its revenue.

C A S E A N A L Y S I S

4. While Raemore clearly is invested in the training of his sales reps, it is difficult to assess the value of the three weeks spent on upgraded product knowledge — if the products are obsolete and out of touch with the needs of the marketplace. It may have been more appropriate to engage the sales force in market research and analysis, including interviews of customers to identify their needs and how well the company meets them.

5. Finally, the case implies difficulty in communicating with Raemore. He may be egocentric in clinging to "his idea"; he may lack vision for the future; and it appears he does not invite his managers to express contrary opinion — or the discussion concerning the connector's obsolescence would have reached a clear and poignant pitch before now. All in all, the New Age Electronics Co. seems to have a leadership problem.

A Few Possible Recommendations the Task Force Might Make ...

1. Conduct a market research study; focus on market segments and the 80/20 distribution of customers; use a reputable marketing expert who can teach in-house staff "new tricks" as they go; make a prototype of both a process and the introduction of a new product for a niche market and run out all the numbers on this market test to demonstrate the strength or weakness of the pilot and what it promises; set goals to reduce cycle time on new product development and introduction; and listen to the customers' assessment of every initiative. They will tell you clearly what they need, how much, why they value it, who your competition is and what they are willing to pay for you to respond to their requirements.

2. Engage the sales force in assessing the problem. Ask them to define the problem as a decline in sales as they know it and to assess their own performance, and recommend to management what they need to attack the problem. Invite the sales force to design their own training program.

3. Initiate a Users Forum for customers, suppliers and a broad representation of people from diverse functions within the company. Seek finely tuned applications for the valuable input you will get from these meetings. Remember, customer satisfaction is at the heart of the Shewhart/Deming Cycle. When companies listen, customers speak.

Deming's 14 Points: Guiding Principles of Total Quality

Deming summarized his foundation work in quality by identifying 14 points for companies to follow. TQM companies enjoy the rewards of practicing these principles.

1. **Create constancy of purpose for improvement of product and service.** Deming suggests companies commit to constant improvement, customer satisfaction, R&D and the development of employees aligned around the company's goals instead of focusing on "quick fixes" for short-term profits. Determine what business the company is in and adapt to the changing needs of the customer. Have a purpose beyond making money. Make that purpose your mission.

2. **Adopt the new philosophy.** Americans have tolerated inferior quality in products and services for a long time. Increased global competition is demanding a shift. Deming challenges companies to approach quality with a new tenacity, in which management and workers are focused on the needs of the customer and in which the commitment to continuous improvement of products and services is constant.

> *"Excellent companies are learning organizations!"*
>
> *Tom Peters*

77

3. **Stop depending on mass inspection.** Deming staunchly advocates the education of workers at every step in the development, delivery and evaluation of the work to troubleshoot the process. American industry has wasted billions making inferior products and in delivering services that have lost customers, only to spend billions more trying to correct the errors and win customers back.

   Typically, "inspection" has had negative overtones and occurs in isolation after the work is done. Deming recommends eliminating inspectors and rewarding people for finding errors, stopping the process and improving both the process and quality as work is performed.

4. **End the practice of awarding business on the price tag alone.** Deming recommends new thinking in vendor relationships. Instead of awarding work on the lowest bid, which often means the lowest quality, companies need to develop long-term relationships with suppliers — some as sole-source suppliers — for any one item. Expect vendors to demonstrate their own TQM. View vendors as business partners and develop mutual respect, trust, responsibility and rewards. Institute a Vendor Certification Process.

   Time spent at the front end in identifying the goal, planning and selecting a strategy to serve all the customers, and clarifying roles and responsibilities will reduce cycle times and errors. Building strategic, reciprocal alliances with suppliers who deliver results over time is a key competitive advantage.

5. **Constantly improve the system of production and service.** Quality requires ongoing commitment to continuous improvement, elimination of waste, and reductions in cycle times. Management achieves this by rewarding the creativity and initiative of employees who try new things and who accomplish benefits for customers and gains for the company.

6. **Institute training.** Deming insists many performance problems can be traced to the lack of orientation and training programs. Management needs to set expectations for employees and demonstrate how workers can be successful in their jobs. Companies must also train their suppliers in new work methods. People want to do a good job. Give them the tools.

7. **Institute leadership.** Managers need to lead people and manage things. Managers need to support workers to their fullest potential and adopt the roles of "coach," "mentor" and "cheerleader." The organization is in the business it's in, but managers are in the organization business — and that means developing people. A manager's final product is creating an environment in which people can make their best contributions — which result in the organization being successful and the customers being satisfied.

8. **Drive out fear.** Three small words, but perhaps the most potent challenge for management to achieve. Deming correctly declares that the companies who make it "unsafe" for employees to ask questions and to take responsible risks are facing tremendous economic losses on the way to their own obsolescence. Employees who are afraid are not free to create. If employees are not free to create, they cannot meet changing customer needs.

9. **Break down barriers between staff areas.** Deming points out the integrity and good sense of why divisions, departments and units need to communicate and work closely with one another. Concurrent design (a standard in Japan) is increasing in recognition in the United States because of its essential contribution to quality, customer satisfaction and profit.

In the service industries, this concept can be applied by integrating planners, systems designers, marketers, financial analysts and customers when services are being developed and process flows are being detailed. Weigh out value price (what the customer perceives as having value and is willing to pay for) and value cost (what it costs the company to produce the service or product). Employees will enjoy collecting this data and making recommendations.

> *"Leadership is working people up."*
>
> *Valarie A. Zeithaml*

79

10. **Eliminate slogans, exhortations and targets for the workforce.** Deming rejects hype and superimposed targets, claiming they have no meaning unless they evolve from the workforce. Deming is opposed to competition within, between and among units of the same organization, believing that kind of competition works against the goal of removing internal barriers.

   Frequently, "hype" is employed to foster competition within the company to produce higher productivity and profit. Deming says organizations need to redirect the competitive spirit to their real competitors on the outside.

11. **Eliminate numerical quotas.** This is a difficult concept to grasp. Everyone knows that business runs on numbers! Translated to a functional definition, this means that achieving the numbers alone does not mean achieving quality, or maintaining or expanding market share, or providing for innovation in new products and services.

   Workers who are held to meeting quotas are held to yesterday's standards; they are not moving the company into the future. Worse, quotas merely guarantee that workers will do whatever it takes to make the mark. This thinking is probably directly responsible for the United States' high defect rate in the past because of its commitment to mass production.

12. **Remove barriers to pride of workmanship.** It is management's responsibility to listen to workers and to determine the barriers that interfere with their good performance. Deming places a great amount of emphasis on management's role to provide an environment where employees can excel consistently. Training for managers and for all employees throughout the organization, providing technology and materials that support the accomplishment of strong results, and instituting a recognition and reward system that supports worker dedication and achievement are essential elements.

Education

13. **Institute a vigorous program of training and retraining.** Adopting a quality program (process) will not be easy or quick. The ideal is for the entire organization to be educated in the new methods, including teamwork and statistical techniques.

    Communicating, planning in a group context, negotiating and problem-solving are areas where training occurs early. Deming advises that training occur top-down at all levels of management first, to assure that managers and supervisors are aligned behind the same concepts and share a common language. Then, those in work groups or project teams on the pilot quality effort are trained in the new methods, teamwork and statistical techniques.

    However, many departments and project teams commit to these same principles. Change occurs at every juncture and has an impact when awareness and practice increase. Management and co-workers will notice improvements — especially, ones that deliver the results they want.

    Because a commitment to quality is a commitment to improvement, companies rethink who they are and how they want to do business. Typically, for most organizations, this is a painful process. It requires insight about one's role in current practices and relationships. New learning and continuous training accompany the route toward continuous improvement.

14. **Take action to accomplish the transformation.** Deming recommends that a special top-management team develop a plan of action to carry out its quality mission. Total quality is a process that recognizes the total organization as a system including all internal and external parties — customers, suppliers and competitors. When the people who comprise the core of the company and its partners understand the 14 Points and the Seven Deadly Diseases, they will become aligned and committed to quality.

> *Total quality is a process that recognizes the total organization as a system including all internal and external parties.*

Deming's Seven Deadly Diseases

Companies frequently run into trouble of their own making. Deming suggests there are "Seven Deadly Diseases" that a company suffers at its own hand. By identifying these traps in advance, a company can save itself a lot of pain and malfunction. Ultimately, customers are the true winners from efficiently run and quality-driven companies.

1. **Lack of constancy of purpose.** When a company has no constancy of purpose, no long-range plans exist, management and employees are insecure and customers are often confused. Everyone wonders what they are supposed to be doing. What is the plan for staying in business? For what purpose is the business organized? This information is significant throughout all departments and in every work group of a company. Managers and supervisors provide a key interface between the company and its workers.

2. **Emphasis on short-term profits.** U.S. business is focused on quarterly reports of profitability that undermine quality and productivity. This obsession has created the misplaced preoccupation with making companies appear to be profitable on paper while neglecting the "big picture" in the long run.

   Financial managers move into CEO positions, and the inventors/innovators of the industry must submit worthy proposals to financial *Wunderkinds* to see — not if the product or process is worthy — but if the numbers work for the next quarter's printout. The goal needs to be reversed: the financial experts need to discover ways to make things possible for R&D, improvements and the long-term financial well-being of the company.

3. **Evaluation of performance by merit rating or annual review of performance.** Deming believes these measurements have the opposite impact on morale and productivity for both managers and workers. They promote fear, inequities, internal competition, anger and discouragement.

4. **Mobility of management.** Managers change jobs because they become discouraged with the companies for whom they work. Because managers are not given the "big picture," they become disenchanted with what they are trying to accomplish. The organization loses its historical memory and the talent once hired to create its future.

5. **Running a company on visible figures alone.** Deming explains that some of the most important figures for a company are "unknowable," including the multiplier effect of a happy or unhappy customer, lost revenue caused by the absence of that "extra mile" by motivated managers and workers that would make all the difference, and the hours of rework saved by front-end planning and communicating. A well-run company depends on more than figures to satisfy customers.

6. **Excessive medical costs for employee health care that increase the final costs of goods and services.** Companies have documented big savings in premiums when prevention takes a front seat in employee health care patterns. Wellness programs, smoking-cessation clinics, health club memberships and regular medical checkups are frequent factors cited in studies demonstrating how companies have saved money through the introduction of various initiatives for employees. When a company saves employee costs, it can create products and services that are affordable to the customer.

7. **Excessive costs of warranty, fueled by lawyers who work on the basis of contingency fees.** Companies that commit to quality and error-free work realize savings during a warranty period with very few nonanticipated services. Quality requires companies to get out in front of customer needs and to understand and diminish variance through continuous improvement. Good customer relationships at every point in the process assure a partnership approach; keeping costs down and delivering services that customers value at a price they are willing to pay are the rewards for doing business by listening to the customer.

> *Quality requires companies to get out in front of customer needs and to understand and diminish variance through continuous improvement.*

Deming's Obstacles

Deming cautions that the "road of continuous improvement" is never-ending. Companies become fatigued and look for shortcuts to quality, but there are none. Deming identifies the following most common obstacles that companies use to reject TQM.

- **"We want overnight success."** Deming cautions against those who believe improvement of quality and productivity are achieved suddenly by affirmation of faith. The transformation Deming speaks of is a deliberate and time-intensive process and will likely require a shift in culture — the essence of a company's values, principles and goals. Repeat: There is no "quick fix."

- **"Investing in new technology will transform our industry."** Not by technology alone will organizations achieve their goals. Commitment to develop the new workforce, to listen to the evolving needs of customers and to maintain dependable relationships with suppliers and distributors begin to capture input from the human side of enterprise. The future includes both high tech and high touch.

- **"Give us a road map."** Companies that look for a "road map" to follow instead of planning their own route to quality will be disappointed. One company's process cannot be superimposed on another organization. Yet, it is beneficial for companies to talk with others that have traveled along the TQM curve to hear to what they have learned.

- **"Our problems are different."** Managers may reject the experiences of other companies as not relevant to their own. Although solutions need to be individualized for each organization, the problems and discoveries of others can provide encouragement and useful insights.

There is no "quick fix."

84

- **"Our quality control department takes care of all our problems of quality."** Stated simply, quality cannot be "assigned" to a department. Total quality is a process, not a program. To achieve total quality, everyone needs to participate in a daily process with deliberation and innovation.

- **"We installed quality control."** There is no end to total quality. It is a way of life where individuals make daily commitments to continuous improvement and cross-functional teams work diligently to achieve incremental results. Total quality is not a light bulb that is turned on and off. Think of it as a whole powerhouse that energizes an entire company.

- **"It is necessary only to meet specifications."** Strict compliance will guarantee keeping up with only yesterday's standard. To move into the future, one must recognize that it may be necessary to go outside the spec to produce innovations that produce higher quality and reduce costs.

How Do I Measure Up on Deming's 14 Points?

Rate yourself according to how strong you are in implementing behaviors that reflect each of Deming's 14 Points. Be sure to review the section entitled "Deming's 14 Points: Guiding Principles of Total Quality" to be clear about Deming's intent for each point. Rate yourself a 1-5 according to the following scale. The highest score you can receive is 70 (14 Points x 5). Note what action step you can take to improve in each of Deming's 14 Points ... write it down and try it out!

1 — **No effort and no opportunity to develop action**

2 — **Minimal effort and minimal opportunity to develop action**

3 — **Moderate effort and moderate opportunity to develop action**

4 — **Advancing with evidence of some continuous improvement**

5 — **Setting the standard in a continuous-improvement mode**

1. Create constancy of purpose for improvement of product and service.

    1   2   3   4   5

    Action Step: _____

    _____

2. Adopt the new philosophy.

    1   2   3   4   5

    Action Step: _____

    _____

3. Stop depending on mass inspection.

    1   2   3   4   5

    Action Step: _____

    _____

4. End the practice of awarding business on the price tag alone.

    1   2   3   4   5

    Action Step: _____

    _____

5. Constantly improve the system of production and service.

    1   2   3   4   5

    Action Step: _____

    _____

6. Institute training.

   1   2   3   4   5
   Action Step: _____
   _____

7. Institute leadership.

   1   2   3   4   5
   Action Step: _____
   _____

8. Drive out fear.

   1   2   3   4   5
   Action Step: _____
   _____

9. Break down barriers between staff areas.

   1   2   3   4   5
   Action Step: _____
   _____

10. Eliminate slogans, exhortations and targets for the workforce.

    1   2   3   4   5
    Action Step: _____
    _____

11. Eliminate numerical quotas.

        1   2   3   4   5

Action Step: _____

_____

12. Remove barriers to pride of workmanship.

        1   2   3   4   5

Action Step: _____

_____

13. Institute a vigorous program of training and retraining.

        1   2   3   4   5

Action Step: _____

_____

14. Take action to accomplish the transformation.

        1   2   3   4   5

Action Step: _____

_____

JOSEPH M. JURAN

Joseph Juran (1904-) may be closest to Deming in his approach to quality. They differ on how difficult it is for a company to achieve quality, how important statistical methods are and whether competition is good or bad. Deming believes achieving quality requires "transformation" and a change in organizational culture; Juran believes an organization can manage for quality.

Juran knew Shewhart at Western Electric and is less impressed with statistics than Deming. Juran views statistical methods as a tool and understands both their merits and limitations. He believes quality starts with knowing who the customers are and what the customers need. Producing goods and services targeted to the right niche markets with the most appropriate technology is no easy accomplishment. Juran agrees that management's commitment to customers, suppliers and employees are at the core of quality. Juran's definition of quality has expanded over the years since his first visit to post-war Japan. Juran defines quality as "fitness for use" including product/service features desired by the customers, with assurance of "freedom from failure."

By the time Juran made his first visit to Japan in 1954, after the publication of his *Quality Control Handbook* (1951), the Japanese were trained extensively in Statistical Methods. They wanted to understand management's role in quality. The Japanese Union of Scientists and Engineers (JUSE) invited Juran to teach them management's responsibilities. In *Out of Crisis* (1986), Deming praised Juran for his work: "His masterful teaching gave Japanese management new insight into management's responsibility for improvement of quality and productivity."

Juran points to three imperatives for total quality to take hold in a company:

- Commitment and action from top management
- Training in Total Quality Management
- Quality improvements at an unprecedented rate

QUALITY =

$$\frac{\textit{Frequency of deficiencies}}{\textit{Opportunities for deficiencies}}$$

J.M. Juran

Quality has improved in the United States but not at a rate comparable to the lead of Japan. Juran speaks about a need for a "revolutionary rate of improvement." It is true that Juran and Deming's ideas are very close indeed. The global marketplace is setting new standards in excellence in both product and processes — both influencing lower costs for the customer.

Juran was honored in 1981 by the Japanese with the award of the Second Order Medal, just as Deming had been recognized in 1960. As a credit to Juran's impact, Japan has more information on Quality Control than any other nation: JUSE published 660 books on quality control between 1960 and 1985. In 1987, Tokyo University ran 520 courses for 48,560 students in Total Quality Control (TQC). Juran has developed a series of videotapes entitled "Juran on Quality," available through the Juran Institute in Wilton, Conn. Juran founded the institute in 1979 and transferred leadership of it to Blanton Godfrey (formerly of AT&T) in 1987. Juran still consults and advises at the institute.

The Juran Trilogy

The **Juran Trilogy** (a trademark of the Juran Institute, Inc.) identifies three areas for quality conversion within a company:

- Financial Planning becomes Quality Planning
- Financial Control becomes Quality Control
- Financial Improvement becomes Quality Improvement

The Juran Trilogy provides a conceptual framework that demonstrates how the quality function can be organized for maximum effectiveness within an organization. The three related functions, while each its own entity, form an interconnected network where organizational processes support the quality function and its goals.

QUALITY PLANNING / QUALITY CONTROL / MANAGING FOR QUALITY / QUALITY IMPROVEMENT

Quality Planning — The focus here is to assure that the goals of quality can be achieved within and through operational activities. Quality-planning activities are those that:

- Identify internal and external customers
- Develop product features that respond to customers
- Establish quality goals that meet the needs of customers at the lowest cost with supplier partners on board early
- Design a process to produce the desired product features
- Demonstrate that the process is capable and that quality goals are met during operations

Quality Control — The objective in QC is to document or certify that quality goals are achieved during manufacturing operations. Quality-control activities seek to:

- Select what to control
- Select units to measure
- Establish measurement methods
- Measure real performance
- Interpret variance, real vs. standard
- Act on the difference between the actual performance and what it should be (the standard)

Quality Improvement — Efforts in this area are geared to push beyond the established norm to create a new standard of excellence. To achieve superior performance, operational quality must also be superior. Quality-improvement activities are ones that:

- Identify specific projects for improvement
- Organize to guide projects
- Organize for diagnosis, discovery of causes
- Diagnose to find causes
- Provide corrective and preventive action
- Prove these remedies are effective
- Provide control to hold the gains

To achieve superior performance, operational quality must also be superior.

91

When Juran first introduced the Trilogy, many companies created separate departments that managed planning, control and improvement. Companies also sought to have suppliers adopt the same quality standards and replicate the three functions within their operations.

Today, TQM companies develop the mind-set toward quality and train people throughout the organization to improve all processes and systems that the company operates. The area of supplier quality assurance is critical for core companies to meet customer requirements.

Juran is credited as the first person to measure the cost of quality. He successfully demonstrated to management what potential increases in profit would occur if the costs of poor quality were lowered. (Feigenbaum further advanced this reasoning with the "cost of nonconformance" argument.)

Juran believes managing for quality is not as easy as Phil Crosby thinks it is, but certainly not as difficult as Deming believes it to be. He does concede most quality programs fail in companies because they do not understand how difficult it is going to be to develop new processes. Still, Juran explains that quality — like finance — can be managed.

Quality — like finance — can be managed.

Juran's 10 Steps to Quality Improvement: Directives for Management

Companies eager to practice TQM often get bogged down in the rhetoric of each of the gurus. Lists of quality principles are mounted on walls throughout a company. Juran provides an action-oriented approach to managing for quality. After each of "Juran's 10 Steps to Quality Improvement," there are practical suggestions for you and your company to put into effect.

1. **Build awareness for the need and opportunity for improvement.**

   Take the risk! Push yourself to identify how you can improve and ask someone for help. Take another kind of risk, and learn how to point out areas that need improvement by asking others what they think and how they could improve the process. If no one ever says, "This needs to get done better!", it never will. Learn the art of sharing constructive comments and invite others to do the same. Promote open, direct and focused communication; be sensitive and respect the feeling and sincere efforts of others. Learn how to coach one another along the continuous-improvement process.

2. **Set goals for improvement.**

   Be deliberate and communicate your goals out loud. Write them down. Anticipate succeeding at each goal. Envision that success; draw mental pictures of what success looks and feels like. Talk it up with the people with whom you work. What are their own goals and visions of success? Start talking about what you can do together. How much more powerful is your vision of success when you combine your efforts? When you add more and more people from your area and other departments, the energy and commitment increase. When you set goals that require collaboration among several function areas, you will find a core of supporters from the beginning.

3. **Organize people to reach the goals.**

You are on your way. You have everyone psyched up just by talking about and envisioning success, which became sweeter because more people were organized around a common goal. That is the secret to getting people involved. They have to begin to link their dreams with those around them. Energy and good spirit in stretching for a goal are infectious.

4. **Provide training throughout the organization.**

Organizations today are revamping the notion of training. Training isn't something that is done to you — a surprise package of new skills you receive by simply attending a seminar. It may begin there, but it is your responsibility and that of your company to apply the new skills and to design ways to measure the impact of change on the productivity and quality of the business.

Training prods new behavior by exposing us to new insights about ourselves, our industry, our customers, technology, teamwork and our communication. We can even be guided through new processes by which we learn to frame problems differently, and then we can learn new ways to solve problems. TQM organizations see themselves as learning organizations. The leadership creates an environment where people are encouraged to be their naturally curious selves. Innovation and risk-taking are nurtured and rewarded; new learning is captured and the institutional memory is a living, breathing video forever moving on fast-forward.

> *Training prods new behavior by exposing us to new insights about ourselves, our industry, our customers, technology, teamwork and our communication.*

94

Training is a continuous process and occurs in a myriad of ways — coaching, mentoring, team learning during projects, individual-development programs, developing a pilot program or evaluating an existing one. Companies have renewed commitment to training because they see it as an investment, not as an expense. Advances in technology and changes in the marketplace are so rapid that companies know they need to employ people who love to learn and who will reinvent a process they just created because they have a better idea! In our globally competitive world, training, learning and inventing are key.

5. Carry out projects to solve problems.

Learning is the focus here. No part of any job should be done on "automatic pilot" within the framework of continuous improvement. People learn by doing, creating a process as they are discovering another one. That is what you did in the Case Exercise using the Shewhart/Deming Cycle.

6. Report progress.

Keeping people informed about the status of your work is a key element to enlisting their support. Although you may not always know whose eyes are on you, you can direct your information to people you want to know about your work. Measurement will demonstrate progress along a continuum. Point out exemplary "quantum leaps" to supplement regular progress.

7. Give recognition.

In a recent survey, senior vice presidents of a major corporation were asked to rank a large number of incentives from an active brainstorming session where 267 factors were itemized. A simple "thank you" for one's effort was first choice for 63% of the respondents. Everyone is busy and the "to do" lists are endless; yet, everyone appreciates recognition and will continue to deliver the best when good work is noted.

*SUCCESS
breeds
SUCCESS.*

95

8. **Communicate results.**

   Make something of that market-research analysis you worked on for the past three months and let people know what you found out and what the possible impact of the new information may be. See how many ways you can probe the next question to be answered; who else can you interest in working on the problem; who else needs to learn what you are finding out; what do you need to know to advance the project to the next rung? If you never talk about the results, people will think you wasted your time and their money. Don't be shy — tell people what you are finding out and ask them to get involved.

9. **Keep score.**

   Measure progress and assess overall progress along a curve. Identifying variance will lead you to demonstrating "how much improvement" and "how much value" over what time and cost. While numbers do not tell the whole story, they play a very significant part in the control of variance and the demonstration of continuous improvement.

10. **Maintain momentum by making annual improvement part of the regular systems and processes of the company.**

    Companies can provide special recognition by acknowledging several strategies or adjustments that improved its systems or processes in a dramatic way. Companies may wish to sponsor annual or biannual "Improvement Awards" to draw attention to the daily gains that lead to every cumulative success. Perhaps, among the many attributes critical for the success of an idea, an individual, a department or a company, is the care that people typically contribute daily to their jobs. Nothing pleases an employee more than when people can see the aggregate impact of his or her work on the success of a company in satisfying customers with high-quality products and services. Maintaining the momentum can be the hardest task of all if no one is with you; or it can become the easiest when people understand and believe in you and your mission.

Joseph M. Juran, ed.
Quality Control Handbook
McGraw-Hill, 1951

"Maintaining the momentum can be the hardest task of all if no one is with you; or it can become the easiest when people understand and believe in you and your mission."

J.M. Juran

ARMAND FEIGENBAUM

Armand Feigenbaum (1920-), founder of General Systems in Pittsfield, Mass., in 1968, is credited with grabbing the attention of corporate leaders by advancing the "cost of nonconformance" approach as a rationale for a commitment to quality. He elevated the importance of expenditures for initiatives that are pitched to achieve higher quality by demonstrating geometric ROI. Further, he has made the argument that those companies that are practicing Total Quality Management are setting the international standards for quality in their industries.

At 24, Feigenbaum was General Electric's top quality expert. He understood that the achievement of quality is the result of a total orchestration of the entire stream of inputs. He discovered "quality was not a group of individual techniques or tools; instead, it was a total field." By integrating the planning, implementation and evaluation of processes among various contributors, Feigenbaum achieved higher quality.

In 1961, Feigenbaum's *Total Quality Control* was published. His views on work-process flows began to push through the isolation of earlier Quality Assurance (sampling and inspection) methods. Feigenbaum realized that whenever he gained improvements on a process within GE, everything in the organization began to improve.

People were energized by improved systems and methods. They fed on one another's successes because Feigenbaum understood systems theory and created an environment that could learn from its own experience. His leadership led to cross-functional team work and an open work environment that provided some of the footprints for focus groups and improvement teams.

"The customer defines quality."

Armand Feigenbaum

Feigenbaum believes the customer defines quality. Deming disagrees to some extent. Deming advises that the real edge comes to the companies that learn their customers so well that they can anticipate the future needs of customers. The companies that are not in touch with those needs simply will not stay in business.

Feigenbaum offers convincing proof of his view about delivering quality to customers with his point on the cost of nonconformance. In a 1988 General Systems' consumer and industrial-markets survey, eight out of 10 buyers put quality ahead of price in their decision to buy. In 1979, it was three out of 10.

Feigenbaum is a staunch advocate of the American worker. Having traveled and worked in numerous countries around the world, he affirms that the American worker has no equal "when given full and necessary support and leadership from management." Feigenbaum is very optimistic that U.S. companies will achieve expansive results with TQM as long as management is committed to the heart of the matter — customers, suppliers and employees.

> *"All employees should feel like winners."*
>
> *Armand Feigenbaum*

Armand Feigenbaum's Six Key Points

Armand Feigenbaum breaks down quality principles into logical and sequential action steps. Although he identified 40 such steps in his *Total Quality Control* (McGraw-Hill, 1961), the six listed here provide insight into key concepts that distinguish Feigenbaum from the other gurus.

> *"What gets measured, gets done."*
>
> **Mason Haire**

1. Total quality control may be defined as an effective system for integrating the quality-development, quality-maintenance and quality-improvement efforts of the various groups in an organization so as to enable marketing, engineering, production and service to function at the most economical levels that allow for full customer satisfaction.

2. In the phrase "quality control," the word "control" represents a management tool with four steps:

   a. Setting quality standards
   b. Appraising performance to these standards
   c. Acting when the standards are exceeded
   d. Planning for improvement in the standards

3. The factors affecting product quality can be divided into two major groupings:

   a. The technological (including processes)
   b. The human

   Of these two groupings, the human is of greater importance by far.

4. Quality control enters into all phases of the industrial-production process: starting with the industrial customer's specification and the sale to that customer; through design, engineering and assembly; to shipment of the product, installation and field service for a customer who remains satisfied with the product.

5. Operating quality costs are divided into four different classifications:

   a. **Prevention costs,** which include quality planning and other costs associated with preventing nonconformance and defects.

   b. **Appraisal costs,** or the costs incurred in evaluating product quality to maintain established standards.

   c. **Internal failure costs,** caused by defective and nonconforming materials and products that do not meet the company quality specifications. These include scrap, rework and spoilage.

   d. **External failure costs,** caused by the defective and nonconforming products reaching the customer. They include complaints and warranty product service costs, costs of product recall, court costs, liability penalties and loss of market share.

6. An important feature of a total quality program is that it controls quality at the source. An example is its positive effect on stimulating and building up operator responsibility for and interest in product quality through measurements taken by the operator at the work station.

A.V. Feigenbaum
Total Quality Control
McGraw-Hill, 1961

> *"An important feature of a total quality program is that it controls quality at the source."*
>
> *Armand Feigenbaum*

PHILIP CROSBY

Phil Crosby (1926-), the first U.S. corporate Vice President for Quality at ITT in the 1970s, is recognized as the guru who brought Total Quality to the boardroom and off the shop floor. He is pragmatic and straightforward and translates complex concepts into language business people understand.

Crosby's *Quality Is Free*, published in 1979, has sold over 2 million copies and is available in several languages. In the book he quotes then ITT chairman Harold S. Geneen: "Quality is not only right; it is free. And, it is not only free, it is the most profitable product line we have."

Crosby created the Zero Defect movement at Martin Marietta in the 1960s. He popularized the slogan "Do it right the first time" — first used at Western Electric in the mid-1930s.

After working in quality for a number of years — studying Deming and Juran — and working through quality control and quality assurance, Crosby was frustrated with the ongoing existence of defects. He disagrees with Deming and believes Zero Defects can be achieved. Crosby rejects statistically based quality methods that accept as inevitable the assumption some things will go wrong at some time. All other quality experts think Crosby is wrong about his concept.

Crosby began to focus on prevention. He pressed management as to why they accepted the statistical theory that a few things will always be bad. He argued that "it must be cheaper to do things right the first time." Management at Martin Marietta needed to hear this logic. Given the critical nature of their work with the government in delivering precision each and every time with complex technology for the military, Crosby's viewpoint placed him front and center on the quality stage.

Crosby has a large organization, Philip Crosby Associates, Inc., with a staff of 325 people located in six states, as well as in London, Paris, Munich, Genoa, Toronto, Singapore, Sydney and Tokyo.

> *"Do it right the first time."*
>
> *Philip Crosby*

Crosby has worked with more than 1,500 companies. People attend his schools to learn about his 14-Point Program — of which there are four basics that he calls the Four Absolutes of Quality Management.

Crosby's approach is pragmatic and energetic. He is alone among all the quality experts in believing that achieving quality can be relatively easy. He has been credited with providing a clear voice with a distinct message on quality that U.S. business is finally coming to understand. Deming thinks Crosby oversimplifies what is really necessary for companies to do in order to achieve TQM. They both agree with the rest of the experts that statistical analysis is a very small part of the whole. The emphasis is on people.

Crosby's Four Absolutes of Quality Management

Crosby holds four guiding principles to serve as his Absolutes of Quality Management. If companies put into practice systems to achieve results reflecting any one of these absolutes, improvements will occur. When a company fully embraces all four absolutes, it is confronting quality imperatives head-on. Results will exceed projections.

1. **The definition of quality is conformance to requirements.** Frequently, this is misunderstood to mean conformance to specifications. Crosby believes the final product or service in a TQM environment reflects 10% conformance to specifications and 90% response to what the customer wants.

2. **The system for causing quality is prevention.** In order to reduce costs, inspection needs to be eliminated. In a TQM organization, the system itself must produce quality on its own. Companies must develop employees to understand the whole job and troubleshoot the system for improvements at every stage.

When a company fully embraces all four absolutes, it is confronting quality imperatives head-on.

3. **The performance standard for quality is Zero Defects.** Crosby believes that the statistical laws promote the myth that defects are inevitable. He simply believes companies can perform at a Zero Defect rate. None of the other experts believe this is even a possibility.

4. **The measurement of quality is the price of Nonconformance.** Crosby added on to the work Feigenbaum had done at GE and demonstrated with hard numbers that it costs more not to produce quality than it does to produce it. The experience of TQM companies holds this Absolute to be true.

Crosby's 14 Points

Crosby's 14 Points are action steps for companies to take in implementing TQM. Crosby takes a very pragmatic approach in making each of these points value-producing for the companies who practice them.

1. **Management Commitment.** To make it clear where management stands on quality. Crosby challenges management to become crystal clear in its focus and strategy and to center its quality efforts around the needs of customers.

2. **Quality Improvement Team.** To run the Quality Improvement Process. The process is continuous and so are the improvements in maintaining a quality edge.

3. **Measurement.** To provide a display of current and potential nonconformance problems in a manner that permits objective evaluation and corrective action. A company needs to understand its baseline and control variance.

4. **Cost of Quality.** To define the ingredients of the Cost of Quality (COQ) and explain its use as a management tool. The real COQ problems arise when the company is not focused on quality methods and results.

A manager should "walk the talk."

5. **Quality Awareness.** To provide a method of raising the personal concern felt by all employees toward the conformance of the product or service and the quality reputation of the company. Training in TQM principles and practices is key.

6. **Corrective Action.** To provide a systematic method of resolving forever the problems that are identified through the previous action steps. Quality at the source empowers people to intervene at any step of the process.

7.9. **Zero Defects Planning and Zero Defects Day.** To examine the various activities that must be conducted in preparation for formally launching Zero Defects Day. To create an event that will let all employees realize, through a personal experience, that a change has occurred.

8. **Employee Education.** To define the type of training all employees need in order to carry out their role in the Quality Improvement Process. Pilot programs provide a viable way for organizations to introduce an integrated process from which "new learning" is captured and translated to other parts of the company.

10. **Goal-Setting.** To turn pledges and commitments into action by encouraging individuals to establish improvement goals for themselves and their groups. Setting targets brings people together to work toward the same end.

11. **Error Cause Removal.** To give the individual employee a method of communicating to management the situations that make it difficult for the employee to meet the pledge to improve. Crosby notes that management needs to understand the experience of its workers to provide supportive work environments structured to deliver the results it wants.

*A better way
every day.*

12. **Recognition.** To appreciate those who participate. People need recognition for their efforts. Managers report that it is the "simple thank you" that makes the difference.

13. **Quality Councils.** To bring together the appropriate people to share quality-management information on a regular basis. Councils are one way to keep quality and its benefits at the forefront of running our companies.

14. **Do It All Over Again.** To emphasize that the Quality Improvement Process is continuous. Quality is never thought of as a "project" with a beginning, middle and end. Quality requires a dynamic process, responsive to new requirements and standards.

KAROU ISHIKAWA

Karou Ishikawa, an aristocrat who died in 1989, graduated from Tokyo University in 1938 and is probably the best known of the Japanese quality gurus. Ichiro Ishikawa, Karou's father, was president of JUSE (Japanese Union of Scientists and Engineers) and the Federation of Economic Organizations. He encouraged the Japanese and his son to accept the message brought to them by Deming and Juran.

Ishikawa was already talking about statistical methods of quality control to the Japanese in 1949. Ishikawa was recognized for his unique contributions in quality when he was awarded the Deming Prize in 1952. Americans visited Japan in the early 1970s to learn about Quality Control Circles and the impact they were having on productivity in Japanese industry; it was Ishikawa who began them in 1962. He was very successful in enlisting senior Japanese management to listen to the suggestions that came out of the Quality Circles (QCs) and in allowing the QCs their autonomy to solve problems.

QUALITY IMPROVEMENT

American managers liked the idea of Quality Circles because they shifted responsibility to American workers. However, American senior management never trusted them enough to allow them their full impact. When the Americans observed QCs in Japan, they did not understand "where" the circles fit in the structure. Crosby explains that since QCs are more a process than a form and because Americans couldn't actually "see" them in a Japanese organization, they didn't know how to import them to the United States.

Ishikawa credited Deming with introducing quality control to Japan in 1950 and also recognized both Shewhart and Juran. Ishikawa believed at first there was too much emphasis on statistical methods, but he was very encouraged after Juran's visit in 1954, which focused on management processes and identified Quality Control as a management tool. In *What Is Total Quality Control?* Ishikawa credits Feigenbaum with the concept of Total Quality Control (TQC). However, Ishikawa believes that Feigenbaum was misguided when he placed TQC as a function of the Quality Control Department and Quality Control specialists. Ishikawa presents the following evidence of his view of organizations and the contributions he expects workers to make: "Since 1949, we have insisted on having all divisions and all employees become involved in studying and promoting QC."

Crosby and Ishikawa agree on some of the basics. Top management needs to provide continuous support and leadership and to serve as a role model for employees in their commitment to quality. Top management needs to set standards and measure individual and group initiative and results in these broad areas. Top management has the main responsibility for poor quality. Both men agree quality improvement will reduce costs. Crosby wants to show management the cost of not producing quality; Ishikawa wants to show everyone.

Ishikawa defines the customer as whoever gets your work next. He was the first quality expert to actually focus on internal as well as external customers. He understood process and the fact that process flowed through people. More than anyone, early on, he formed the notion of a shared vision and unifying all people in an organization around that vision,

> *"The customer is whoever gets your work next."*
>
> *Karou Ishikawa*

107

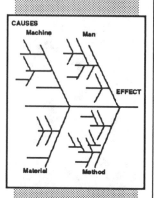

CAUSES
Machine   Man

EFFECT

Material   Method

mission and goal. Ishikawa exemplifies this belief in this statement: "Company-wide quality control cannot be complete without total acceptance of this kind of approach by all workers. Sectionalism has to be broken down, and the company has to be ventilated so that everyone can enjoy a breath of fresh air."

How many American companies need ventilating today?

Case Study: Using a Cause-and-Effect Diagram

Ishikawa introduced the Fishbone Diagram to assist with problem analysis. For every effect or error, one could work backwards to discover fundamental root causes. The Cause-and-Effect Diagram illustrates a systems approach to categorize causes by clustering causal events under the four broad areas of man, method, materials and machine.

Review the following case problem and discuss it with your co-workers. Use Ishikawa's Fishbone Diagram to analyze the problem presented here. A worksheet is provided for you to itemize cause-and-effect factors under the four broad categories of man, method, material and machine. A blank diagram is provided for you to graphically represent your analysis.

Case Problem

Ed Winfield, CEO of One World Semiconductor, was more surprised than anyone when the introduction of the firm's new laptop personal computer failed to achieve its projected recognition and sales. The company had counted on a strong market entrance leading to significant revenue for the next five quarters. Early results indicated only 67% of the expected revenue was achieved. Winfield knew the firm would be in trouble if it didn't discover why its new laptop's introduction had been bungled.

In no particular order, here is the information the Corrective Action Team (CAT) discovered as it asked many questions. Work the Cause-and-Effect Diagram to discover the relationships of the information and their cumulative impact on the introduction of the new laptop.

CAT reached the consensus that the first unwanted "effect" would be identified as "new product introduction failure." There was debate whether or not "failure" was an accurate term because sales did register 67% of projections. In this instance "being off the mark" to such a large extent would make things financially difficult over the next 18 to 20 months and might jeopardize the introduction of the next generation of laptop — the Compulite II. Marketing said that money earmarked for a "product test" was scratched when customer participation/interest was low. Usually, One World had a high participation level during a product test. CAT did a follow-up phone survey to learn "why" people declined to participate in the laptop market test. Most of the individuals who refused to participate in the market test were part of an original customer design team. CAT learned that customers felt their suggestions and concerns weren't taken seriously during the design phase so there was no incentive to participate later.

CAT also discovered that R&D monies to research the full capabilities of the technology were cut in half because of belt-tightening within the firm. When CAT asked "how" decisions were made regarding R&D monies, they discovered there was no record of the decision-making process. Only the results were noted. Next to the Compulite Laptop a 50% reduction in R&D was noted. In addition, the program's lead software engineer was lured to the competition just after the midpoint. Tim Perkins, division manager, kept this from Winfield because Perkins knew they were "past the point of no return."

Perkins hired a highly skilled software engineer to replace the first project manager. The new person found little documentation on developing the new product. Information on customer requirements was particularly limited.

Manufacturing also complained that documentation in the design and lack of specificity regarding customer requirements left them on their own. Time was a factor so they cut a few corners to save time. One of Manufacturing's decisions was to encase the product in a black compartment because the suppliers had that material ready. Consumers gave this color choice a negative rating.

When CAT finally made a full report to Winfield, the CEO then understood that more teamwork and better communication and problem-solving were required at One World. In addition, he saw how important it was to record the decision-making process.

CASE STUDY

109

CASE SUMMARY

Cause-and-Effect Diagram Worksheet

(Fill in the additional causes identified in the case study.)

MAN	METHOD	MACHINE	MATERIAL
1. Lack of incentives	1. Lack of documentation	1. No reliability data	1. Color of material (black) not acceptable
2.	2.	2.	2.
3.	3.	3.	3.

CAUSES

MAN

METHOD

Lack of incentives

Lack of documentation

No reliability data

Poor color choice

MACHINES

MATERIALS

EFFECT
New Product
Introduction Failure

GENICHI TAGUCHI

Genichi Taguchi is best known for the Taguchi Loss Function, which has roots in some of Deming's teachings, and which Crosby believes would be hard to apply in most American companies. The Loss Function demonstrates a formula to determine the cost of a lack of quality. Deming, on the other hand, believes it is impossible to calculate the actual cost of the loss of quality. Taguchi, however, is very serious about the validity of his Loss Function.

The principle states that for each deviation there is an incremental economic loss of some geometric proportion. The cumulative impact can be great for a number of parts deviating just a little. Taguchi's belief is the opposite of the traditional view, which states that there will be no detrimental impact as long as the parts are within the engineering tolerances or specifications. Designing to spec, therefore, when many parts are at the further end of those tolerances, can have an overall negative impact on quality and profit.

The practical application of the Taguchi Loss Function can save a company a lot of money. This method was applied to a transmission of the Ford Motor Co., and its warranty losses were corrected because Ford was able to achieve less variation and therefore greater quality.

Think of this concept in the management of a company. Consider the interrelationships and interdependence among finance, marketing, sales and information systems. Each group has systems and procedures it has developed to achieve its goals. In order for each department to perform optimally, all other work from the various other departments must be understood and incorporated into a flow chart to reflect the integrity of the whole.

Following Taguchi's thinking, if all systems and schedules are off slightly, there may be little impact per individual event on its own department. Taken collectively, the toll will be far greater. If each department missed a deadline by a day or two, the total impact will have greater consequences for the end customer in that chain.

> **Build QUALITY into each increment of product development and production.**

111

Preventive steps demand planning and flow charting in advance among managers and employees to gain a full understanding of goals and responsibilities. Anticipating how the batons are passed, benchmarking and identifying contingency plans are just a few tasks that Taguchi recommends. Cross-functional teams, on-line systems and regular face-to-face communications among all the parties involved in the process chain are also critical.

Taguchi was awarded the Deming Prize in 1960.

The Taguchi Loss Function

The following is an example of the Taguchi Loss Function applied to a fictional company. By examining the impact of the cumulative damage of the errors, you can see how important collaboration, communication and project management are to achieving quality.

XYZ Company was asked recently to examine the cumulative impact of errors made by various departments in fulfilling a customer contract. The contract stated the project had to be delivered within five days of the target date. Although each department had variance within some acceptable range, the total impact cost the company a customer. The concepts of the Taguchi Loss Function are demonstrated clearly by this analysis:

DEPARTMENT	NUMBER OF ERRORS	DAYS LOST TO REWORK	DOLLAR LOSS
Planning	3	2	12,000
Finance	1	—	5,000
Contracts	2	1	1,500
Engineering	2	1	3,000
Software	2	2	5,000
Purchasing	2	1	1,500
Manufacturing	1	1	15,000
Distribution	—	—	—
TOTALS	**13**	**8**	**43,000**

Acceptable Range: 5 days off schedule.

Result: XYZ Company lost a customer and a chunk of its profit on the project.

STATISTICAL CHARTS

The charts included here have evolved from the quality movement over the years. They are simple graphic representations of underlying processes that track variation and guide people to think in logical ways to correct any variations outside of customer satisfaction.

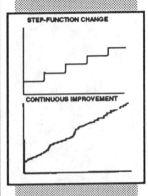

Look at the graphs on the right contrasting Step-Function Change with Continuous Improvement. Step-Function Change represents those events that are planned and methodical. Improvements are sequential, logical and incremental. A system will be operational in a state of equilibrium, only to alter when the next planned change occurs and the system picks up and propels itself to the next rung. There it rests on a plateau until next time.

In contrast, change along the Continuous Improvement chart is less predictable and occurs in smaller increments. However, change and improvement are constants; over time, the gains made are greater than in the Step-Function. There is more fluidity and energy in the Continuous Improvement method because all people in the process-flow change are driving the improvements.

The Seven Basic Tools Charts are described on page 114 and represented graphically on page 115. These charts reflect foundation principles that guide total-quality organizations in problem-solving, measuring and making decisions about improvement processes.

THE SEVEN BASIC TOOLS FOR TQM

1. **Cause-and-effect diagrams** are also known as fishbone diagrams, after their shape, and Ishikawa diagrams, after their originator. They are typically used to depict causes of certain problems and to group them according to categories, often "method," "manpower," "material" and "machinery." (Chapters 6 & 10)*

2. **Flow charts or process-flow diagrams** are the visual representation of the steps in a process. They are particularly useful in the service industries, where the work process involves unseen steps. (Chapters 10 & 12)*

3. **Pareto charts are simple bar charts** used after data collection to rank causes so that priorities can be assigned. Their use gives rise to the 80-20 Rule — that 80 percent of the problems stem from 20 percent of the causes. (Chapter 10)*

4. **Run (trend) charts** show the results of a process plotted over a period of time: for example, sales per month.

5. **Histograms** are used to measure the frequency with which something occurs — how often a train departs 10 minutes late, for example, as opposed to five minutes or 60 minutes late. (Chapter 10)*

6. **Scatter diagrams** illustrate the relationship between two variables, such as height and weight. As points for events are plotted, relationships are determined and similar clusters and deviations are observed. (Chapter 10)*

114

7. **Control charts** are the most advanced of the seven basic tools and are used to reflect variation in a system. They are run charts with statistically determined upper and lower limits. As long as the process variables fall within the range, the system is "in control" and the variation within the range stems from "common cause." The goal is to narrow the range between the upper and lower limits by eliminating the common causes that occur day in and day out. Controlling variation equates to controlling cost and conforming to customer or company requirements. (Chapter 12)*

*Many of these charts are explained throughout this manual.

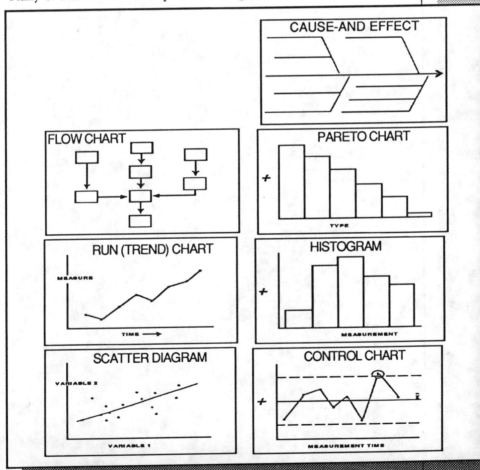

Assessment of TQM Readiness

INTRODUCTION

Once people have been exposed to TQM principles and learn about the success companies are having with practicing TQM, most managers want to know, "OK, where do we start?" An internal sweep of any given company that has not yet embraced its own improvement process will demonstrate a wide range of awareness levels among managers and employees about TQM and its value.

"OK, where do we start?"

From your review of the "TQM Awareness Checklist" in Chapter 1, you focused on a "snapshot" of your company, yourself, and other managers and supervisors with whom you work. That Checklist covers all the main ingredients around which companies begin to orchestrate change programs and continuous improvement processes.

Additionally, your responses to the "TQM Performance Rating" in Chapter 2 gave you further insight in rating your participation in practicing TQM with your customers and your team and within your company's culture.

Guiding Values of TQM

Here is a quick refresher of some of the main values and characteristics reflected in any quality program:

- Customer-driven strategy
- Quality-driven company
- Vision, mission and goals aligned around the needs of the customer and communicated throughout the company
- Clear incentives for innovation and improvements
- High-quality, low-cost product design and production achieved through collaboration with internal, diverse functions, and suppliers engaged as business partners in serving shared markets
- Cross-functional teams at work on continuous-improvement processes
- Open communication, mutual trust and respect are the norm
- Managers committed to training and development for all
- Continual customer interface

When you were rating both your company and yourself on these components, you were receiving some initial feedback about your TQM readiness and that of those with whom you work. You probably were able to identify some gaps between where you are today and where you might like to go — with quality efforts either within your department or within your company as a whole.

The "TQM Awareness Checklist" and the "TQM Performance Rating" provide a framework for you to begin thinking about how you can make an overall assessment of your awareness and practices of TQM principles and methods. The "TQM Organizational Readiness Assessment" may be useful as you and others at your company prepare to practice TQM.

ASSESSING TQM ORGANIZATIONAL READINESS

Quality is becoming a way of life in more and more
organizations around the globe. People are beginning to see
that "quality" is not a trend that has only a very limited shelf-
life. Rather, companies are succeeding by commitment to
quality and all that it requires in terms of investments in
training, R&D, suppliers, new technology, internal and external
customers and employee involvement.

Achieving gains in a competitive marketplace, where TQM
standards are already high, demands aggressive and strategic
determination and follow-through in equipping managers and
employees with the training and tools they need to advance
within a TQM environment. Both Japan, through the Deming
Award, and the United States, through the Baldrige Award,
have provided companies with precise and intense systems of
assessment. The "TQM Organizational Readiness Assessment"
presented here includes many of the criteria used in the
evaluation of companies for each of those awards as well as
for awards administered by many states.

Rate each of your responses to the criteria in the assessment
that will evaluate the quality of your organization as it now
functions according to the following Rating Scale from 1 to 5:

1   No evidence of effort

2   Slight evidence of effort: limited integration in the
    company as a whole

3   Evidence of effective effort: some notable; many
    others lack maturity

4   Evidence of effective effort: many notable; good
    integration within the company as a whole; good
    deployment

5   Continuous and outstanding effort and results:
    effective integration and sustained processes that
    reinvent themselves; national and world leadership

> *"The best
> defense for the
> future is a
> strong offense
> today."*
>
> *Anon.*

TQM ORGANIZATIONAL READINESS ASSESSMENT

PRODUCTIVITY AND LEADERSHIP   (highest possible score: 30 points)

1. **Senior Management Involvement** _____
   The extent to which senior managers of the organization are personally involved in leading the productivity and quality efforts and are supporting members of the organization. Senior managers serve as models in knowing how to "walk the talk."

2. **Strategic Planning** _____
   The extent to which productivity and quality planning are integrated into the strategic planning process.

3. **Productivity and Quality Culture** _____
   The extent to which productivity and quality values have been incorporated into the culture of the organization and have become a "way of life" and a "way to do business." These values should be reflected in written materials, policies, systems and decision-making.

4. **Productivity and Quality System** _____
   The extent to which effective systems and organizational structure exist to achieve productivity and quality improvements, including the quality-improvement process, problem-solving process, measurement systems and statistical process control.

5. **Communications** _____
   The extent to which the organization has effective communication among functional areas.

6. **Supplier Partnerships** _____
   The extent to which the organization has established partnerships with suppliers of materials, equipment, people or information to assure productivity and quality inputs.

TOTAL SCORE FOR PRODUCTIVITY AND LEADERSHIP _____

HUMAN RESOURCE EXCELLENCE (highest possible score: 25 points)

1. **People as a Strategic Resource** _____
   The extent to which people are viewed as a strategic resource and a source of competitive advantage.

2. **Development of People** _____
   Evidence of the continuous development of people to support organizational and individual objectives.

3. **Participation** _____
   Existence of mechanisms and evidence of the use of those mechanisms to achieve participation of individuals in continuous process improvements.

4. **Diversity** _____
   Evidence of actions to create an environment where diversity of talents is recognized as a strength and actions are taken to assure that the diverse talents of individuals are used.

5. **Workforce Readiness** _____
   Evidence of actions to promote workforce readiness such as dependent care, flex-time, flex-place, literacy or language programs and valuable benefits.

TOTAL SCORE FOR HUMAN RESOURCE EXCELLENCE _____

121

PRODUCTIVITY/QUALITY RESULTS (highest possible score: 20 points)

1. **Productivity and Quality Improvement**   _____
    Graphic representations that depict productivity and quality gains
    over at least the last three years. Focus specifically on quality and
    productivity rather than improvements in profitability, increases in
    sales, etc. Demonstration that charts reflect a company's progress
    along the continuous-improvement curve through value added per
    employee, total factor productivity, error rates or defects, cost of
    quality, rework, yield, warranty costs and cycle times.

2. **Innovation**   _____
    Evidence of product or service innovation and speed with which
    new products or services are developed and introduced.

3. **Process Capability**   _____
    Evidence of improvements in process capability for product or
    service delivery.

4. **Benchmarking**   _____
    Evidence of the use of benchmarking to indicate how the quality
    and productivity results compare with industry-based, world-class
    leaders.

TOTAL SCORE FOR PRODUCTIVITY/QUALITY RESULTS   _____

CUSTOMER ORIENTATION AND RESULTS (highest possible score: 20 points)

1. **Customer Requirements**   _____
   Evidence of effective systems for determining and monitoring changes in customer requirements.

2. **Customer Focus**   _____
   Evidence that all individuals view customer satisfaction as a primary task.

3. **Customer Satisfaction Trends**   _____
   Quantitative data showing external customer satisfaction trends over a multiyear time period.

4. **Customer Satisfaction Comparisons**   _____
   Comparison of customer satisfaction ratings with those of competitors, industry averages, etc.

TOTAL SCORE FOR CUSTOMER ORIENTATION AND RESULTS   _____

IMPACT ON COMMUNITY (highest possible score: 15 points)

1. **Economic**   _____
   The economic impact of your quality and productivity-improvement achievements on the state and local community through jobs created, impact on tax base, increased productivity or quality of other organizations, reduced price to consumers, increased services provided and increased client base.

2. **Environmental**   _____
   Evidence that environmental impact is a strategic consideration; actions to prevent or minimize adverse environmental impact.

3. **Productivity and Quality Awareness**   _____
   Evidence of participation in partnerships that promote improvements in the level of productivity and quality knowledge and awareness in the community.

TOTAL SCORE FOR IMPACT ON COMMUNITY   _____

123

TQM ORGANIZATIONAL READINESS TOTAL SCORE

PRODUCTIVITY AND LEADERSHIP (30)   _____

HUMAN RESOURCE EXCELLENCE (25)   _____

PRODUCTIVITY/QUALITY RESULTS (20)   _____

CUSTOMER ORIENTATION/RESULTS (20)   _____

IMPACT ON COMMUNITY (15)   _____

                                        TOTAL SCORE (110)   _____

Interpreting Your Score

The highest possible score you could have received is 110, based on a high of five for each variable evaluated within the criteria clusters. These criteria will again help you frame areas where you need to focus your improvement efforts toward becoming a TQM manager and a TQM company.

Optimize the Value

This assessment can be adapted by your company and used by a number of departments. You may find it interesting to note both similarities and differences in the perception of your organization's effectiveness in the areas of quality and productivity among different respondents.

This assessment also provides an ideal starting point around which organizations can become focused in tackling areas of greatest concern in their improvement processes. It will help you to determine areas of strength and weakness within the company.

> *"The enterprise can decide, act and behave only as its managers do."*
>
> *Peter F. Drucker*

125

*C*HAPTER 8

Preparing for Implementation

INTRODUCTION

Companies and managers eager to improve quality and productivity want the results that TQM can deliver. In thinking about your assessment of readiness, an important question will come to mind: "Where do I start?"

A few key building blocks will help you and your company prepare for the introduction of TQM. It is important to build on the strengths of the organization, letting employees know that this effort is an extension of their positive contributions. The notion is to create an enthusiasm, a passion that spreads to all parts of the organization.

BUILDING BLOCKS FOR TQM IMPLEMENTATION

Two-Way Communication

It would be very difficult to implement TQM without establishing a dialogue between supervisors and employees. This interaction will begin to build trust and confidence necessary for employees to take responsibility for continuous improvement.

Outcomes of positive two-way communications:

- An atmosphere that facilitates open discussions that focus on the needs and concerns of employees.

- A forum for employees to discuss ideas and make suggestions to improve work processes.

- An opportunity to recognize individual and team achievements.

Getting Started

Each department should set up a weekly meeting that should run about one hour. The meeting should be held the same time each week, if possible, with at least one topic planned in advance. The goal is to evolve this technique into an improvement-team process, later described in Chapter 9.

Meeting Topic Suggestions:

- Goals and objectives
- Progress reports
- Problem-solving about work issues
- Work issues and concerns
- Learning exercises
- Training analysis

Suggestion Programs

Suggestion programs do work! Give employees a chance to participate in the improvement process through a formal method of submitting ideas and recognition for those ideas that help the business improve. Consider such ideas as:

- Improving customer service
- Reducing costs
- Eliminating waste
- Increasing safety
- Working smarter

Getting Started

Encourage all employees to submit their constructive suggestions which may have benefit to their department or to the company.

Guidelines for Suggestions:

- Recognize a problem, potential problem or opportunity for improvement.

- Present facts/information that recommend a potential solution or cost savings.

- Submit in written form (see sample suggestion form on next page).

- Sign the suggestion.

Ask a coordinator to log the suggestions and send them to the appropriate department for review. If the suggestion can be implemented, it is recommended that a cash award be presented to the employee for a percentage of the annual estimated savings, not to exceed $1,000. Intangible benefits — suggestions that do not have a definite measure — should receive an award based on perceived value to the company. Awards in this category could be made more frequently and range from $25 to $1,000.

> *"Good companies tell you how they collect employee suggestions. Great companies tell you how they use them."*
>
> *Harvard Business Review*

129

SAMPLE SUGGESTION FORM

1. Describe the present system, condition or process:

2. My suggestion to improve is:

3. Department manager to whom suggestion should be sent:

4. My suggestion will

    ☐ Save processing time
    ☐ Save equipment time
    ☐ Save forms, paper or supplies (attach samples)
    ☐ Save office space
    ☐ Improve safety factors
    ☐ Improve employee morale
    ☐ Other (explain)

    Please send your suggestions to _____. Use additional sheets if necessary. Your suggestion will be acknowledged. Thanks for your ideas!

    Name: _____ Dept.: _____ Phone: _____

TEN WAYS TO GET INVOLVED IN TQM

The most important aspect of any TQM effort is the involvement of every employee. One TQM company published a vision of employee involvement that stated: "Each employee is expected to be the best they can be in their jobs, but also to take actions to improve that job on a daily basis."

The following checklist is a start for you to begin to take immediate action.

1. **Find out why something is being done the way it is.** Think about a way it can be done better, quicker, with less cost.

2. **Be open-minded.** Don't make premature judgments.

3. **Brainstorm.** Use your imagination. Don't reject ideas because they seem silly. A seemingly foolish thought can often lead to a valid one.

4. **Be flexible.** If one approach leads to a dead end, switch to another. Use as many perspectives as possible.

5. **Be selective.** Think to the point.

6. **Be persistent.** Take a shot at the problem each day. If you can't find a solution, forget the problem for a while and return to it later.

7. **Listen to your co-workers' problems about the details of their jobs.** You may be able to see a solution because you're not directly involved.

8. **Make notes.** They could lead to solid ideas later.

9. **Learn from the best.** Someone else's idea may lead to one of your own.

10. **Enjoy it.** The recognition for getting involved is really satisfying.

> *"We do the work; therefore, we must find the answers for doing it better."*
>
> *David K. Carr*

131

FORCE FIELD ANALYSIS

Removing Barriers

Before beginning any major implementation, it is critical to assess where the resistance to change may exist. The idea is to identify where "land mines" may be positioned in your organization prior to initiating TQM goals. The plan is to remove this resistance to change prior to implementation to ensure greater chance of success. It is also important to identify the positive factors at the same time. These positive factors will help support your change and must be reinforced to provide the momentum for the change.

The force field analysis is a tool for analyzing a situation you want to change. It helps you alter conditions that are potential barriers to the success of the implementation.

The method is based on the work of Dr. Kurt Lewin, in which he states that any goal or change issue has both positive (driving) and negative (restraining) forces occurring at any given time.

The plan is to remove this resistance to change prior to implementation to ensure greater chance of success.

132

MODEL

Current Situation

↓

DRIVING FORCES (+)	RESTRAINING FORCES (-)	GOAL/TARGET

→ ←

The technique is to set up the force field analysis prior to beginning the implementation. Removing restraining forces can ensure success.

Let's Look at an Example

Situation: Assume that a product-reject rate has increased to 15% over the past few months. You have decided to complete a force field analysis to try to identify barriers and reduce the reject rate to 5%.

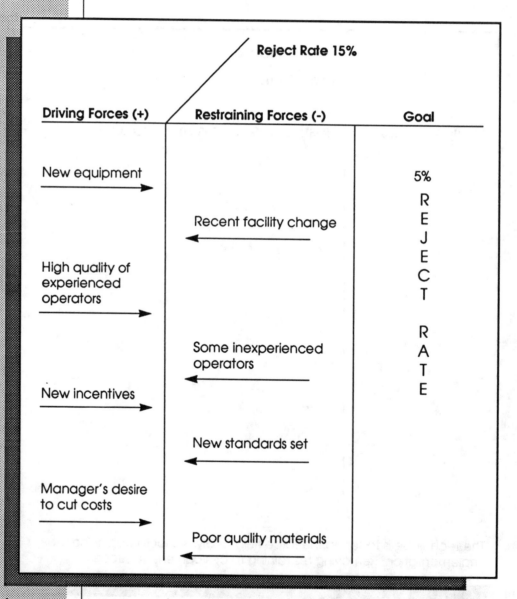

Reject Rate 15%

Driving Forces (+)	Restraining Forces (-)	Goal
New equipment →		5%
	← Recent facility change	R
		E
		J
High quality of experienced operators →		E
		C
		T
	← Some inexperienced operators	
		R
New incentives →		A
		T
	← New standards set	E
Manager's desire to cut costs →		
	← Poor quality materials	

Create an Action Plan to Remove Restraining Forces

It is not enough to identify the driving and restraining forces for implementation. An action plan must be created to list the steps needed to remove the restraining forces.

In the example below, one of the restraining forces listed on the previous page to reduce reject rates was the new standards set. The issue was that these new standards were impeding performance because some employees had not completely mastered them. Here's what an action plan would look like.

Restraining Force: Optimal Performance with New Standards

Action Steps:

1. Review standards with each employee to ensure full understanding of the goals.

2. Identify the gap between each employee's current performance and expectations set by the new standards.

3. Identify possible causes of any anticipated performance: lack of knowledge/skill, lack of tools or lack of motivation.

4. Specify whether individual or group instruction will be needed.

5. Design an appropriate training program.

6. Improve the work area and provide appropriate tools.

7. Adjust incentives if feasible and provide recognition for achievement.

135

FORCE FIELD ANALYSIS EXERCISE

1. Identify a situation that you need to analyze using the force field analysis method.

2. Use the Force Field Analysis Worksheet (opposite) to itemize both the driving (supportive) and restraining (resistive) forces that have an impact on the situation.

3. Create an action plan (page 138) to demonstrate what steps can be taken to position your efforts (alter the environment) toward optimal results in the situation.

FORCE FIELD ANALYSIS WORKSHEET

Your Force Field Analysis: Removing barriers to successful
implementation. List the driving and restraining forces.

YOUR CURRENT ENVIRONMENT

Driving Forces (+)	(Barriers) Restraining Forces (-)	Goal
		T Q M E N V I R O N M E N T

Action Plan to Remove Restraining Forces

Select one restraining force and list the action steps to remove or improve it.

Restraining Force:

Action Steps:

FORCE FIELD ANALYSIS SUMMARY

The Force Field Analysis is most useful when you are starting the implementation of a change or are confused about what step to take next. Some of the benefits you will see immediately include opening up new ideas for action, making the problem manageable and helping individuals or groups to reach consensus.

Just a word of caution. The results depend on the quality and completeness of your analysis. Don't be concerned if the Force Field seems overly analytical. It will ensure success in the long run.

Operating Hints:

1. Define the current (equilibrium) situation clearly and determine the desired end result. Help people to identify as many forces as possible. Stick with it, even though the method may seem a little silly at first. Stick with brainstorming ideas and don't bog down on what can or can't be done.

2. Include information from as many relevant parties as possible. Use flip charts.

3. Test to see whether the analysis includes motivation of influential parties, policies and procedures; the nature of individual needs and habits; outside forces; administrative practices; financial and material resources; etc. After you have completed the analysis, prepare an implementation plan for the proposed change. Include:

   a. The necessary events that must occur
   b. A timetable of events
   c. Names of the relevant people who can help
   d. Responsibility for implementing the subparts
   e. Coordination of the subparts
   f. Provision for feedback and evaluation

> *"Creative problem-solving is the ability to overcome obstacles by approaching them in novel ways."*
>
> *Andrew J. DuBrin*

Training and Development

INTRODUCTION

In order for you and your company to succeed with a total quality management implementation, people and work processes must be improved. The focus of this chapter is to identify the skills and training needs required to create a TQM environment with respect to employees on the "front lines" of the business, as well as the management teams who lead them.

> **"Today's preparation determines tomorrow's achievement."**
>
> **Anonymous**

The real success of total quality rests in your ability to integrate people with technology — processes, systems and equipment (see at right). Whether your business is labor or capital-intensive, success will still depend on how well people respond to problems and challenges, as well as on the quality of their decisions. The training and development focus will be on the tools and skills necessary to create competitive advantage in your employees.

People
- Knowledge
- Skill
- Ability

QUALITY

Technology
- Processes
- Systems
- Equipment

Focus on how you can have an impact on the people side.

141

THE CHANGING WORKPLACE

U.S. companies have been structured in traditional, functional and hierarchical systems for many years. During this time a set of values or culture was developed and reinforced as the way of doing business. Many of these organizations achieved a high level of success by making decisions at high levels, leaving managers and employees to implement their directives. Some management experts described this type of environment as "Theory X," especially emphasized by Douglas McGregor in 1960 in *Human Side of Enterprise*.

Much has changed, and it is still changing at a rapid and sometimes chaotic rate. Pressures of competition, deregulation, regulation, technology, mergers, economy and globalization have created an emerging organizational picture. This new picture or paradigm (set of rules or principles) requires companies to conduct business differently if they are to survive and thrive in the coming decade. The hot buttons that many companies are addressing include:

- Fast cycle times to get new products to market ahead of the competition

- Technical innovation to initiate breakthrough products and services

- A consistently high level of quality to meet and exceed customer expectations

- Customer loyalty to ensure long-term success

If these goals are to occur on a regular basis, what will be needed from the workforce at all levels to succeed? What culture will best support these needs?

Let's look at some of the appropriate changes.

Change the tools that people use. Change the way people feel about work. Change the way work is done.

142

TQM AND MANAGEMENT INFLUENCE

In order for a total-quality culture to evolve, management influence is an essential component. Many believe that this is the heart and soul of any TQM effort. One of the main vehicles of influence is the vision for the company. One of the most famous and compelling visions was established by NASA in the 1960s: "Place a man on the moon by the end of the decade."

This vision was not only achieved in 1969 but created clear direction for all the supporting agencies and departments to focus their work.

The management teams can influence the culture in other significant ways. One additional method would include preparing and communicating the values of the organization as guidelines on how employees are expected to perform and behave, and of course the senior management team would model these values or "walk the talk."

The emerging role of management includes some of the following characteristics:

- Expert at coaching and counseling employees
- Able to create a climate of participation among employees
- Able to delegate responsibility to employees to take action
- Provide training and tools to take more responsibility

Managers should be able to

- Enable employees
- Entrust employees
- Empower employees

The vision of excellence or the "To Be" state.

143

TOTAL QUALITY MANAGEMENT: TQM AS ORGANIZATION CULTURE CHANGE

In moving from the traditional culture to the TQM culture, recognition of specific behaviors and attitudes is essential for initiating a change. Think about your company culture and attitudes and assess your current situation. Consider using the earlier change tool — Force Field Analysis — to initiate a shift in your area.

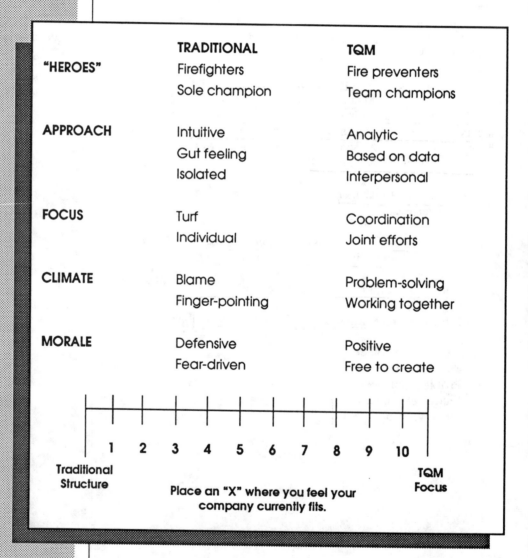

	TRADITIONAL	TQM
"HEROES"	Firefighters	Fire preventers
	Sole champion	Team champions
APPROACH	Intuitive	Analytic
	Gut feeling	Based on data
	Isolated	Interpersonal
FOCUS	Turf	Coordination
	Individual	Joint efforts
CLIMATE	Blame	Problem-solving
	Finger-pointing	Working together
MORALE	Defensive	Positive
	Fear-driven	Free to create

1   2   3   4   5   6   7   8   9   10

Traditional Structure

TQM Focus

Place an "X" where you feel your company currently fits.

144

TOTAL QUALITY MANAGEMENT: A PARADIGM SHIFT IN ATTITUDES

FROM TRADITIONAL:	TO TQM:
Other people are bad and are to be mistrusted.	Other people are good and deserve a climate of trust.
Betrayal and failure are a natural way of life.	Honoring commitments and making relationships work are a natural way of life.
Blame others when things go wrong.	Work together to make improvements when things go wrong.
Concentrate on telling others how they screwed up.	Concentrate on "catching people doing something right."
Life is competitive. Cooperation is the exception.	Life is cooperative. Competition is the exception.
Personal success is measured in competitive terms. For me to succeed, you must fail.	Success is measured in cooperative terms. Success equals "Earning your trust."
Excellence is an idealistic dream.	Once the skills have been mastered, life based on excellence runs more smoothly.
My identity is with my group, not with the organization.	My identity is tied to the entire organization as well as my own group.
Rewards are fixed. If you want your share, you have to compete.	Rewards can grow in size if we cooperate.

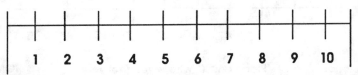

Traditional Structure — 1 2 3 4 5 6 7 8 9 10 — TQM Focus

Place an "X" where you feel your company currently fits.

TOTAL QUALITY MANAGEMENT: HOW THE PARADIGM SHIFT AFFECTS THE COMPANY

FROM TRADITIONAL:	TO TQM:
Excellent quality perceived as too expensive.	Excellent quality understood as the path to lower costs.
Worker jobs strictly defined and limited.	Worker jobs include responsibility for continuous improvement.
Worker training narrowly focused on specific job tasks.	Worker training broadly focused on analytic skills and problem-solving.
Low work standards, frequent punishment for failure.	High work standards, coaching and training given to ensure success.
Customers angry with product failures.	Customer satisfied with reliable, high product quality.
Customers switch companies often, out of frustration.	Customers develop long-term relationships with companies — who have sole-source partnerships with their suppliers.

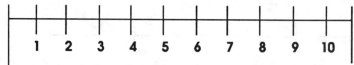

| | 1 | 2 | 3 | 4 | 5 | 6 | 7 | 8 | 9 | 10 | |

Traditional Structure

Place an "X" where you feel your company currently fits.

TQM Focus

THE NEW ROLE OF MANAGERS

TQM requires an environment that has a shared responsibility for goal-setting, problem-solving, feedback and continuing development. One of the most effective methods for a manager to create this environment is by improving coaching skills. This is the most positive way to begin to empower employees to take on more responsibility.

Complete "The Manager as Coach" self-assessment and scoring sheet. As a result, you may want to establish self-improvement goals to enhance your coaching skills.

MANAGER AS COACH
Coaching Practices

Instructions: For each statement below, decide which one of the following answers best applies to you. Place the number of the answer in the box at the left of the statement.

5. Usually   4. Often   3. Sometimes   2. Occasionally   1. Rarely

1. ☐ I keep my team members informed about our overall organizational plans and operating results.

2. ☐ When I ask my team members to accomplish something, I specify the end result wanted rather than how to do it.

3. ☐ I keep my team members informed on how they're doing on the job.

4. ☐ I provide support and backing to my team members.

5. ☐ I express my displeasure and concern to my team members whenever they don't achieve expected results.

6. ☐ I am accessible to my team members and easy to talk to, even when I am very busy and under pressure.

147

7. ☐ I have thorough discussions with my team members to help them learn from their successes and failures.

8. ☐ I talk with my team members about their ambitions and aspirations for the future.

9. ☐ I encourage my team members to participate in setting goals and in determining how to achieve those goals.

10. ☐ I insist that my team members think through problems and make important decisions on their own.

11. ☐ When I talk with my team members about their performance, I am open and frank in telling them what I think.

12. ☐ I provide encouragement to my team members whenever they are undertaking difficult assignments.

13. ☐ I praise my team members whenever they achieve a significant result.

14. ☐ I empathize with my team members' viewpoints when I discuss problems and undertakings with them.

15. ☐ I provide opportunities for my team members to broaden their experience and increase their competence.

16. ☐ I explain to my team members the requirements they would be expected to meet to qualify for larger responsibilities within our organization.

17. ❑ I clarify with my team members their duties, responsibilities and the important results they are expected to accomplish.

18. ❑ In working with my team members, I follow up on just the significant teams rather than on all the various minute details.

19. ❑ I work with my team members in developing agreed-to "standards of performance" to use in judging the results they have achieved.

20. ❑ I contribute ideas such as tactics, strategies and approaches to my team members for the results they have achieved on the job.

21. ❑ I provide appropriate recognition and rewards to my team members for the results they have achieved on the job.

22. ❑ I encourage my team members to express themselves openly, even when their views differ from mine.

23. ❑ I chat with my team members about the ways they might improve their effectiveness on the job.

24. ❑ I discuss with my team members specific things they might do to better qualify themselves for taking on greater responsibilities in the future.

LEADERSHIP PRINCIPLES

"Sayings of Nemoto"

Masao Nemoto, managing director of Toyota, initiated several efforts to implement Total Quality Control in his company. Over the years, he composed several principles that he used to instill the goals of quality in Toyota managers.

ANALYSIS SHEET FOR COACHING PRACTICES

Instructions: Place the number you selected in the box at the left of each statement. Work down the sheet. Next, add the numbers across, for each set of three boxes, to determine your totals. Add your totals column to obtain your Grand Total.

ACTIVITY				TOTALS
Goal-Setting	☐ 1. +	☐ 9. +	☐ 17.	= ☐
Delegation	☐ 2. +	☐ 10. +	☐ 18.	= ☐
Performance Feedback	☐ 3. +	☐ 11. +	☐ 19.	= ☐
Providing Assistance	☐ 4. +	☐ 12. +	☐ 20.	= ☐
Motivation	☐ 5. +	☐ 13. +	☐ 21.	= ☐
Working Relationship	☐ 6. +	☐ 14. +	☐ 22.	= ☐
Continuing Development	☐ 7. +	☐ 15. +	☐ 23.	= ☐
Future Growth and Advancement	☐ 8. +	☐ 16. +	☐ 24.	= ☐

Grand Total ☐

A manager's overall effectiveness in coaching can be determined by his or her score in the Grand Total box as follows:

Score Range	Overall Rating
101 - 120	Excellent
81 - 100	Good
61 - 80	Fair (needs some improvement)
60 or below	Poor (needs improvement in many areas)

Scores for each set of actions: Specific areas for improvement can be determined by analyzing the scores for each of the eight sets of activities. A score of 10 or less in any set indicates an area for further consideration.

These principles may be useful to you in assessing how you focus on key factors that influence quality improvement. They are summarized as follows:

1. **Improvement after improvement.**
   Focus on continuous improvement and create an environment that will encourage employees to initiate process improvements.

2. **Coordinate between divisions.**
   Break down the barriers between divisions, departments and subsidiaries. Cross-functional coordination is key.

3. **Everyone speaks.**
   Encourage participation. Employees' ideas and views are important to the success of the business.

4. **Do not scold.**
   Avoid giving criticism and punishment when mistakes are made. Take the opportunity to engage employees in corrective action. Much learning will occur.

5. **Make sure others understand your work.**
   Managers must be skilled in teaching and making presentations. This is a method of building collaborative and productive relationships.

6. **Send the best employees out for rotation.**
   Offer training and skill upgrades to productive employees. This is a good method for building company loyalty and long-term commitment.

7. **A command without a deadline is not a command.**
   Without deadlines, tasks are much less likely to be completed.

> *"The manager is the dynamic, life-giving element in every business."*
>
> *Peter F. Drucker*

151

8. **Rehearsal is an ideal occasion for training.**
Preparing to make presentations is a great opportunity
to practice and learn new techniques. This is a good
employee-development tool.

9. **Inspection is a failure unless top management
takes action.**
Immediate action must be taken as soon as a problem
is identified. Management must be active in the
problem-solving process.

10. **Ask subordinates, "What can I do for you?"**
Employees take active roles in briefing management in
routine, informal meetings about quality improvements.

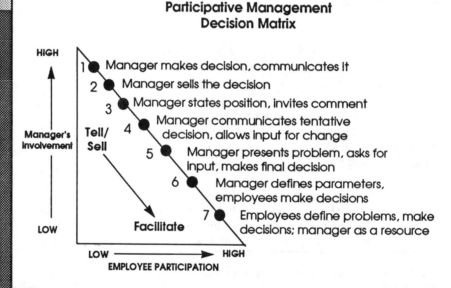

Participative Management Decision Matrix

HIGH

1 — Manager makes decision, communicates it

2 — Manager sells the decision

3 — Manager states position, invites comment

4 — Manager communicates tentative decision, allows input for change

5 — Manager presents problem, asks for input, makes final decision

6 — Manager defines parameters, employees make decisions

7 — Employees define problems, make decisions; manager as a resource

Manager's Involvement — Tell/Sell — Facilitate

LOW

LOW ──────▶ HIGH
EMPLOYEE PARTICIPATION

Circle the number that is your predominant style of decision-making. It
is suggested that, as employees become skilled in problem-solving, a
manager becomes a facilitator as indicated in 7.

How will your decision style affect your company's business?

DEMING'S 14 POINTS APPLIED TO MANAGEMENT

For each of Deming's 14 Points, review the corresponding implications and then note what you are actively doing to implement each of the points. Give yourself and your department a star (*) for those areas where results are being measured and linked to specific initiatives. Check (✔) areas that require your immediate focus.

Point	Implication	How I Measure Up
1. Create constancy of purpose for the improvement of product and service.	Redirect role of supervision from "checking on employees" to encouraging ideas, innovation and improvement suggestions. Develop strategies for maintaining quality standards.	
2. Adopt a new philosophy.	Develop and reinforce a commitment to excellence in workmanship and service.	
3. Stop depending on mass inspections.	Shift attention from inspection for defects and compliance to emphasis on improving the process.	

153

Point	Implication	How I Measure Up
4. End the practice of awarding business on lowest price.	Develop long-term relationships with suppliers and vendors that ensure highest quality at fair prices. Develop confidence in moving materials from loading dock to stock.	
5. Continuously improve the system.	Establish an attitude of seeking quality improvement throughout the system. All jobs, all departments.	
6. Train, train, train.	Ensure that employees have skills for the job today and in the future.	
7. Be a leader.	Develop skills to motivate, inspire and influence employees. Be an environmental creator.	
8. Eliminate fear.	Shift from the traditional punishment for mistakes to mutual respect and understanding.	

Point	Implication	How I Measure Up
9. Break down barriers between departments.	"We" vs. "them" must end. Develop communication between departments. It must start with supervisors and managers.	
10. Avoid fads and fanfare.	Catchy sayings and T-shirts won't do. Instill pride and teamwork to get the best job done.	
11. Eliminate quotas.	Develop sound baseline measure for quality and productivity. Work to improve them.	
12. Remove obstacles to excellence.	Provide the tools and resources for employees to do the job. Coach and motivate. Empower employees.	
13. Provide quality education programs.	Develop a quality vision and share it with employees. Provide training on use of improvement tools, charts, etc.	
14. Get involved in the transition.	Take the initiative — don't wait for someone to "push" quality. Go after the tools and techniques. Active vs. passive posture.	

155

THE NEW ROLE OF EMPLOYEES

In this approach to TQM, teams, not individuals, are responsible for overall performance. As companies become flatter and managers have larger spans of control, the improvement team is the most powerful unit in ensuring successful operations.

As a result of more emphasis on teams, a requirement for team development has emerged. The following checklists and tools will help to strengthen this critical element of team effort. First, some ideas on how you personally apply the continuous-improvement principles (below). Second, some ideas on how a team forms and becomes productive.

These checklists and tools contain some of the key methods to achieving TQM. When combined with effective problem-solving tools in Chapter 10, increases in productivity become immediately apparent.

APPLYING CONTINUOUS IMPROVEMENT PRINCIPLES
Personal Growth Requires:

FOCUS AREA	How Do You Measure Up? (Place an "X")		
	Often	Sometimes	Never
1. Recognizing opportunities to develop new skills.			
2. Establishing objectives that stretch your ability.			
3. Having confidence in yourself.			
4. Making effective use of time, money and resources.			
5. Having a future vision.			
6. Interacting well with co-workers.			
7. Allocating time for work, family and self.			
8. Placing team goals above individual goals.			
9. Willing to make sacrifices for the success of your team.			

Ideas to continuously improve:

_____

_____

MAKING TEAMS WORK

It seems that no matter what your job responsibilities include, participating in some team activity is almost a sure thing. Companies are using many different types of teams, some of which include improvement teams, project teams, task forces and quality circles. Although their specific goals may vary, these teams are trying to use the same collective problem-solving abilities of team members.

The process of forming teams and making them work in a productive and results-oriented way requires key elements to ensure success:

- Clear roles
- Skill development
- Participative environment

The most successful teams have been able to create a synergy that has led to impressive results. If the key elements are prepared in advance of team formation, a much higher degree of success is possible.

Role of the Team Leader

The role of the team leader is focused in three areas:

1. **Preparing for the Meeting.** This essentially focuses on preparing an agenda in advance of the meeting to ensure that the team is clear about what is to be accomplished. The leader should also designate the meeting format, such as "Share information" or "Problem-solve," so members will be prepared to participate.

2. **Leading the Meeting.** The team leader is responsible for guiding the team toward its goal by keeping the meeting on track. The leader may need to deal with team interaction problems such as conflict or dominance among members.

> *"To find out how to improve productivity, quality and performance — ask the people who do the work."*
>
> ***Harvard Business Review***

157

3. **Follow-up.** Quite often, action items must be accomplished to ensure the goals are met. The team leader is responsible for assigning specific tasks and monitoring their completion.

Guiding Principles

The team should establish three key principles that will help the team interact in a positive manner:

1. Nurture and develop self-esteem by establishing a positive and supportive environment.

2. Focus on key issues, not people.

3. Ensure that feedback and follow-up occur as a result of the team's output.

Role of the Team Member

It is essential that everyone on the team gets involved in the team meetings through the following:

- Making suggestions for topics
- Brainstorming ideas
- Supporting the team leader
- Making a commitment to follow-up

Training for team members should be a regular part of the process.

Problem-Solving

The heart of any improvement team is the ability to engage in a systematic problem-solving process that both identifies and analyzes all aspects of the problem. The team leader and team members should be knowledgeable in the basic problem-solving tools mentioned throughout this manual.

Brainstorming — the act of speaking before thinking.

TEAMS

An improvement team works directly on improving processes, such as finding better ways of doing things and eliminating waste. The net result is improved productivity. List the characteristics of the best and worst teams you've belonged to.

Characteristics

Best Teams:

_____

_____

_____

_____

Worst Teams:

_____

_____

_____

_____

Our goal is to create the best teams. Exemplify the "best" characteristics and eliminate the "worst" in your teams to improve productivity and customer satisfaction.

Use these characteristics to review your company's meetings.

TEAM LEADER SKILLS CHECKLIST

The success of any team resides to a large degree in the skills of the team leader. This individual is responsible for team orientation, meeting planning and process. To assess your current skill level, whenever you identify a need for a refresher or development, an action plan should be initiated to enhance current skills.

Review the list of skills below and note your own effectiveness in each area by assigning an S, D or R based on the following description of ability:

(S) A strength, some experience
(D) A development need
(R) Refresher would help

1. Recruiting and selecting team members (optional) _____
2. Scheduling, planning and conducting team meetings _____
3. Keeping the team focused on the problem-solving process _____
4. Assisting the team in obtaining the information and resources needed for problem-solving _____
5. Working with a facilitator to train team members _____
6. Assisting the facilitator in documenting team progress _____
7. Getting team-member involvement (maintain/encourage group participation) _____
8. Clarifying role of team members and objectives _____
9. Knowing how to handle conflicts _____
10. Being able to communicate team's progress to management _____
11. Establishing milestones to measure team progress _____
12. Knowing basic problem-solving tools _____

TEAM LEADER DEVELOPMENT PLAN

To create your own Team Leader Development Plan, list those skill areas where you rated yourself either as a D (development need) or R (refresher). Then brainstorm ways for you to improve your ability in each skill area. Note how and when you will evaluate yourself again to see what progress you have made (#1 is a sample).

Skill Area/Rating (D,R)	Actions to Improve	Progress Check	Target Date
1. Knowing how to handle conflicts (D)	1. Seminar or short course	1. Within 1 month	____
	2. Read *Getting to Yes*	2. Within 3 weeks	____
	3. Select a "coach" who will model effective skills	3. Within 1 month	____
	4. Volunteer at mediation center; get training	4. Within 1 month	____
	5. Identify a conflict and begin to work on it, using new inputs	5. Within 5-6 weeks	____
		Evaluation:	
		1. Feedback from instructor and tests	____
		4. Feedback from mediation trainer and clients	____
		5. Feedback from other people in the process; reduction of conflict	____

161

TEAM LEADER DEVELOPMENT PLAN

Create your own Team Leader Development Plan.

Skill Area/Rating (D,R)	Actions to Improve	Progress Check	Target Date
1.			
2.			
3.			
4.			
5.			

TEAM MEMBER SKILLS CHECKLIST

One area overlooked for development is the team member. For many employees the skills needed to be successful in an improvement-team environment may be new, possibly because they have been working in a traditional culture, where they are usually told what to do. The following checklist can be utilized prior to a team formation and after the team has begun its activities.

For the team to be effective, the leader or supervisor must commit to team-member development.

Fill out the checklist. Where refreshers or development needs are indicated, prepare an action plan to schedule required activities.

(S) A strength, some experience
(D) A development need
(R) Refresher would help

1. Participating in team meetings through:
   - Listening actively
   - Offering suggestions   _____

2. Communicating with team members during and after meeting   _____

3. Following up on assigned action items   _____

4. Highlighting the positives and progress being made   _____

5. Resolving conflicts among team members   _____

6. Interacting with employees and managers whom you don't know   _____

7. Placing the team's goals as top priority   _____

8. Influencing other employees to get involved   _____

TEAM MEMBER DEVELOPMENT PLAN

To create your own Team Member Development Plan, list those skill areas where you rated yourself either as a D (development need) or R (refresher). Then brainstorm ways for you to improve your ability in each skill area. Note how and when you will evaluate yourself again to see what progress you have made (#1 is a sample).

Skill Area/Rating (D,R)	Actions to Improve	Progress Check	Target Date
Example:			
1. Following up on assigned action items	1. Force Field Analysis of demands on my time	1. Within 1 week get consensus where necessary	_____
	2. Prioritize areas of importance	2. Within 2 weeks list should be shorter!	_____
	3. Set deadlines for top priorities and link completions to rewards (6-month to 1-year action plan)	3. Within 3 weeks written action plan	_____

TEAM MEMBER DEVELOPMENT PLAN

Create your own Team Member Development Plan.

Skill Area/Rating (D,R)	Actions to Improve	Progress Check	Target Date
1.			
2.			
3.			
4.			
5.			

Tools for Problem-Solving All Employees Should Know

INTRODUCTION

As an increasing number of companies begin to implement the concept of employee empowerment, the need for employees to know more and do more on the job becomes critical. At the heart of this transition for employees is their ability to identify and solve problems related to the individual job or to the improvement of a work process.

THE PROBLEM-SOLVING STAGES

Stage 1: Explain the situation and define the problem. Establish an improvement goal.

>   **Tools:** Brainstorming
>   Flow charting

Stage 2: Understand the situation by collecting and analyzing data.

>   **Tools:** Check sheet
>   Cause-and-effect diagram
>   Pareto chart
>   Scatter diagram
>   Histogram

> *"Deliberation should be joint; decision single."*
>
> ***Peter F. Drucker***

167

Stage 3:   Identify solutions and implement an action plan.

Tools: Force Field Analysis (Chapter 8)

The other tools are described in detail in this chapter.

BRAINSTORMING — A USEFUL TECHNIQUE FOR GENERATING IDEAS

Brainstorming is an excellent technique for generating ideas from team members about problems and opportunities for improvement. It allows everyone to participate and is a good method for "breaking the ice." This group process can be productive because group members can use their collective thinking power to create and build on the ideas.

Some reasons why brainstorming increases the team's ability to generate ideas:

- Increases involvement and participation
- Produces the most ideas in the least amount of time
- Reduces the need to give the "right" answer
- Reduces possibilities of negative thinking

Some basic ground rules:

- **Don't criticize or evaluate ideas.** That comes later.

- **Go for volume.** The greater the number of ideas, the greater the possibility of good ones.

- **Encourage combining ideas or "piggybacking."** It is a great opportunity to merge ideas or build on them.

- **Encourage participation.** One way is to ask each member, in turn, to contribute an idea. If they have none, they can "pass."

- **Document the ideas on a flip chart.**

Ten heads are better than one.

When using brainstorming as a technique for generating ideas, it is important to focus on the improvements. When the brainstorming list is completed, the group should reach consensus by identifying the top two or three ideas that will help them reach the improvement goal. This may be accomplished by removing obstacles or spending additional time in problem-solving.

FLOW CHARTING

The most effective use of flow charting is identifying the steps and obstacles that a product, process or service follows to completion. As the flow chart is developed, you can identify steps that may be required or unnecessary, duplicative or of low value. Decisions can easily be made to improve the workflow by eliminating wasteful steps.

Flow charts provide valuable documentation and show the interrelatedness of the steps to completion. Your employees may find flow charting useful in looking at the various tasks that make up their jobs, with the opportunity to reduce both cycle and processing times.

Ideal Use: A departmental team meets to draw a flow chart of its work process. Once the current steps are plotted, the team discusses opportunities to create a more efficient work process. In coordination with you or another supervisor and/or team leader, the group can decide on a plan to implement necessary adjustments.

Key Symbols:

⊂ ⊃	Start or stop
↓	Direction of flow
☐	Process step
◊	Decision point
⇓	Movement between locations
○	Evaluation point

For an example of flow charting, see the Socio-Technical Systems section of Chapter 12.

> *The most effective use of flow charting is identifying the steps and obstacles that a product, process or service follows to completion.*

CHECK SHEET

Check sheets are most effective when you need to prepare data based on observations, with the goal of detecting patterns of problems or defects.

Check sheets are most valuable to you in identifying exactly what is occurring and **how often** it is occurring. They provide a systematic method for making observations.

Setting up the Check Sheet:

Agree on the time frame and specific events (behaviors) to be observed.

List: Problems Patterns	Time Frame Weekly/Monthly, etc.					
	Mon	Tue	Wed	Thu	Fri	Sat
(1)	# of occurrences 卌		I	I	II	
(2)						
(3)						
(4)						
(5)						
(6)						

Sample Check Sheet

Problems: Customer Complaints	Week One					
	Mon	Tue	Wed	Thu	Fri	Total
On hold too long	⃉ I	II	IIII	I	⃉ ⃉ I	24
Rude operator	II	I	I	I		5
Question not answered	III	II	II	⃉	I	13
Product not available	I	⃉	I			7
TOTAL	12	10	8	7	12	49

The check sheet will show the patterns of problems and the number of occurrences so that you are able to investigate and improve this situation.

CAUSE-AND-EFFECT DIAGRAM

Cause-and-effect diagrams help to focus on different categories of causes, which provides an excellent tool for grouping and organizing efforts to improve a process. When the major causes of a quality problem are determined, data collection and analyses become much more targeted to understanding what is necessary to improve the process.

Cause-and-effect diagrams are most valuable when you need to identify and display the causes of a problem.

This process, often referred to as Ishikawa's "Fishbone Technique," creates a meaningful relationship between an effect and its possible causes.

For each effect there may be several major categories of causes. To group these causes, the 4 M's were established*:

- Machines
- Manpower
- Materials
- Methods

*It may be appropriate to use other categories.

Constructing a Cause-and-Effect Diagram

STEP 1
Draw an arrow to the box called Quality Characteristic. Select the effect that you would like to diagram.

Quality Characteristic

STEP 2
Add 4 categories (machines, materials, methods, manpower).

MACHINES   MATERIALS

METHODS   MANPOWER

Quality Characteristic

STEP 3
Add the causes of the effect.

MACHINES   MATERIALS

METHODS   MANPOWER

Quality Characteristic

172

Use of Cause-and-Effect Diagrams

Cause-and-effect diagrams are a tool of analysis used most effectively when integrated in a total problem-solving process. When combined with other methods and tools — brainstorming, Pareto charts, flow charts, scatter diagrams, etc. — the richness of the analysis deepens and areas for some of the best improvements are identified.

1. Compare every possible cause with current procedures.

2. Prioritize the impact of causes and select the key ones for improvement.

3. Brainstorm solutions and reach consensus.

4. Implement improvements once solutions have been agreed upon.

5. Keep a record of the diagram as a reference point.

6. Revise the diagram after improvements are implemented.

PARETO CHART

Pareto charts are most effective when you need to show the relative importance of problems. It can help to select a starting point for problem-solving or to identify the underlying cause of a problem.

The Pareto chart is essentially a bar graph that depicts the types and quantities of problems.

"Plans are nothing. Planning is everything."

Dwight Eisenhower

> *"You must identify a problem before you can solve it."*
>
> *Andrew J. DuBrin*

Sample Pareto Chart

Strategy is to work on the tallest bar.

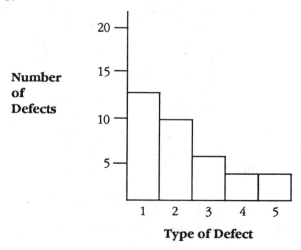

Number of Defects

Type of Defect

Sources for Pareto chart input:
- Check sheets
- Brainstorming lists
- Existing department reports

Getting Started:

1. Identify the problems for charting.
2. Select the unit of measure; e.g., cost, frequency.
3. Select the time frame for data collection.
4. Construct the Pareto chart and graph data.
5. Make corrective action on the tallest bars and improvements should begin.

174

Check Your Understanding

Refer to the chart below. Which problem occurs most often and approximately how often does it occur?

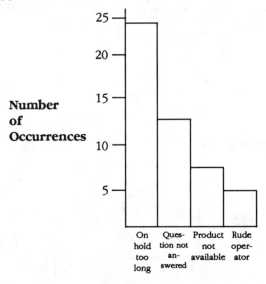

Number of Occurrences

| On hold too long | Question not answered | Product not available | Rude operator |

Customers waiting on hold too long occurs most often. This problem occurs approximately 25 times (a week).

Note: The sample check sheet on page 171 was a means for gathering information. A Pareto chart is one means of displaying this information and presenting findings to management.

SCATTER DIAGRAM

Scatter diagrams are most effective when you want to determine the strength of the relationship between two variables and to display what happens to one variable as the other changes. By using the Scatter technique, the strength of the variables' relationship will become evident.

A horizontal axis is used to display the values of Variable 1, and the vertical axis is used to display the values of Variable 2.

> *"Most organizations measure customer satisfaction by how well they avoid customer dissatisfaction. A common mistake is if few customers complain, most are happy."*
>
> *David K. Carr*

175

Sample Scatter Diagram

The direction and closeness of the cluster identify the strength of the relationship. If both variables move in the same direction, a positive correlation may exist. If variables move in opposite directions, a negative correlation may exist.

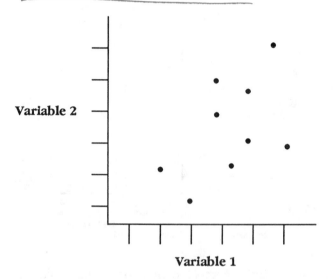

Constructing and Interpreting a Scatter Diagram

STEPS

1. Select two variables to examine the strength of their relationship. (Example: number of training hours related to manager performance level)

2. Determine the values for each variable. (Example: quantify hours and quality levels)

3. Plot the values of each variable on the corresponding vertical and horizontal axis. (Example: elements are individual managers)

4. Identify the strength of the relationship between the two variables for each element charted. (Example: analyze the impact of the numbers of training hours a person has received and his or her effectiveness as a manager)

5. Review the performance of individual elements in
    relationship to all other elements being charted against
    the same two variables. You will see the average
    performance of the group and make some
    observations about variance among elements in the
    cluster. (Example: make a statement about the impact
    of the number of training hours and the average level
    of performance as it reflects the effectiveness of all the
    managers as a whole)

Sample Scatter Diagram

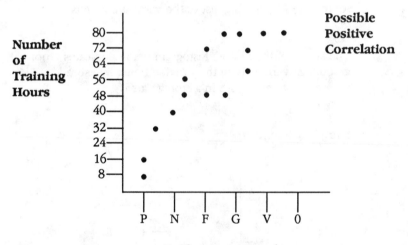

**Number
of
Training
Hours**

80
72
64
56
48
40
32
24
16
8

P   N   F   G   V   O

Performance Level

**Possible
Positive
Correlation**

P - Poor
N - Needs improvement
F - Fair
G - Good
V - Very good
O - Outstanding

A picture is worth a thousand words.

HISTOGRAM

Histograms are most effective when you need to identify and display the distribution of data through bar graphing the number of units in each category. The histogram shows specific measurements and their distribution. The value of the histogram is to show the amount of variance within a process and to identify a problem with the process if a normal bell-shaped curve is not reflected in the data.

A histogram is, in effect, a graphic means to represent any frequency data you may have collected.

The frequency of occurrence of any given measurement is represented by the highest of the vertical columns on the graph.

The shape of the sample histogram below indicates a normal amount of variability in the variable being measured. (Example: temperature in a storage area)

Sample Histogram

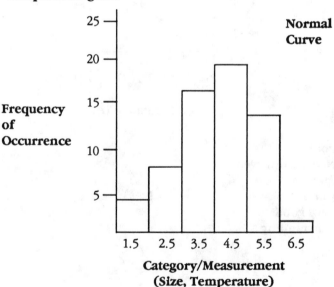

The shape of the following histogram represents a large amount of variability in the variable being measured.

Sample Histogram

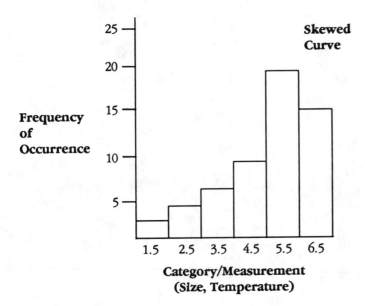

**Category/Measurement
(Size, Temperature)**

> "… Where order
> in variety we see,
> and where,
> though all things
> differ, all agree."
>
> *Alexander Pope*

Measurements

INTRODUCTION

Meeting customer requirements is the ultimate measure of quality. At every step along the fulfillment chain of service to the customer, measurements provide data that indicates how precise a company is in its managerial and operational processes. Anything the company does that does not provide value for the customers by meeting their requirements is viewed as waste. So, measurements play a vital role in determining how efficient and effective a company is in serving the customer.

> "There is only one valid definition of business purpose: to create a customer."
>
> *Peter F. Drucker*

Customer-Supplier Chain

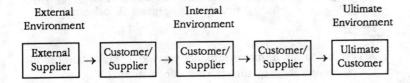

181

Unless a company, department or you make a commitment to measure the impact of actions, there will be no evidence to identify progress along the path of continuous improvement. To locate where the errors are occurring and with what frequency and to decide what interventions are most effective in correcting particular problems, you must use measurements.

Measurements provide critical feedback to you and to the company on how effective and efficient the company is at meeting its goals related to such priority concerns as:

- Customer satisfaction
- Financial targets
- Market strategies
- Process improvements
- Product/service features
- Quality and costs of poor quality
- Human resource development

Companies use measurements internally to assess actual performance against established baselines of performance for individuals, departments, business units and teams. Baselines identify the internal view of excellence and enable companies to set targets for continuous improvement. Even as departments meet current baseline expectations, they are breaking through the measurement grid creating new ones.

To achieve a broader view of performance excellence, companies benchmark with other companies for external baselines of "Best Practices" among leaders in their own as well as other industries. Benchmarking strengthens companies for world-class competition in both product and process quality. David Kearns, former chief executive officer of Xerox Corp., defines benchmarking as "the continuous process of measuring products, services and practices against the toughest competition of those companies recognized as industrial leaders."

According to Juran, measurements provide a "higher precision for communicating quality-related information ... Vague terminology is unable to provide precise communication. It becomes necessary to 'say it in numbers.'" The increasing complexity of our techno-industrialized society requires such commitment and reportage.

Measurements are needed in every area where performance and results directly and vitally affect the survival and prosperity of the business.

182

Measurements are applied to determine valued product/service features and process distinctions as well as deficiencies. Total quality companies make a vigorous commitment to measurement to:

1. Assess current performance
2. Set goals for improvement
3. Understand what is important

The financial impact of all deficiencies presented as one number is known as the Cost of Poor Quality (COPQ). Juran, Feigenbaum and Crosby have spent considerable effort demonstrating to management why it needs to know COPQ. From a purely financial standpoint, COPQ becomes the strongest rationale for a company to commit to continuous improvement: the Cost of Poor Quality consists of those costs that would disappear if a company's products and processes were "perfect."

The investment a company makes in determining what variables are important to measure is essential for the company. Both the customers' perspective and the information that measurement provides a company about its performance make the critical difference in whether that company stays in business. Both internal baselines and external benchmarks are important guides for a company in its pursuit of continuous quality improvement.

The rapid rate of the introduction of new technology combined with increasing global competition has created a quickly changing and uncertain business environment. Staying close to the customer means delivering highest value for best cost; and although measurements are expressed in numbers, those numbers must reflect a measurement of some value of quality that endears your customer's loyalty.

> *"Employees do what management inspects, not what management expects."*
>
> *James Robinson*
> *CEO - Am Ex*

RATIONALE FOR USING MEASUREMENTS

The introduction set the stage for why companies need to commit to measuring what they do. The goal of all measurement is to meet customer requirements in delivering the highest quality for the "Best Cost." Measurements keep companies focused on continuous improvement according to actual results they achieve in producing products and services as compared to internal baselines and external benchmarks of "Best Practices."

Assessing performance is the only way a company, department, business unit, team or individual knows if each is meeting its mark. And, in today's global marketplace, it is the customer who sets the mark. Knowing how well or how poorly one is meeting specific goals and where one stands in view of the competition drives the continuous-improvement process. Companies must align their business strategy and process capability around their customers' requirements.

Measurements are typically organized around assessing:

1. Major business processes
   — Financial
   — Product quality
   — Process quality

2. Quality and quality-improvement processes

The rationale for using measurements can be summarized according to the following:

1. Meeting customer requirements

2. Meeting (exceeding) the competition

3. Responding to (reducing) customer complaints

4. Continuing to improve quality

5. Reducing the cost of poor quality (COPQ)

> *The goal of all measurement is to meet customer requirements in delivering the highest quality for the "Best Cost."*

CATEGORIES FOR SETTING OBJECTIVES AND MEASUREMENTS

Category	Examples
Financial Growth in market share	15% increase in Eastern region in the next fiscal year
Product Quality Accuracy standards, reject rates	Less than 1% deviation from error rates standard in the next year
Process Quality Reduction in customer complaints	100% customer retention rate
Quantity Number of units produced and sold	Production schedules met on greater than 95% of plan this year
	Achieve 100% of sales quota for product "X" this year
Time Lines Completion within specified times	95% of project completed on schedule this year
	Material planning system installed by 3rd quarter
Quality & Quality Improvements TQM training	Senior team trained this quarter and steering committee tasked and trained next quarter
	Train-the-trainer sessions for 5 steering-committee members

> *"Appraisal of a manager should focus on proven performance."*
>
> *Peter F. Drucker*

185

BASELINE MEASUREMENTS

Baseline measurements are a critical component of the improvement process. They form the anchors or the "stake in the sand" for assessing progress and overall performance toward the stated target or goal. Baselines respond precisely to customer requirements and set standards of excellence throughout the organization in its many diverse departments and for its various processes and functions.

The process for determining the baseline is designed to link the voice of the customer and business plans with both team and individual measurements. To ensure that these links are made, it is the responsibility of management to communicate its expectations clearly. Employees throughout the company need to hear and understand management's business plans and strategies. Management needs to explain how important the work of each employee is to the success of the company.

Customer-driven companies are populated by people who are committed to continuous improvement. They work diligently to achieve incremental improvements and develop new baselines as a routine part of the way they work to reflect changing needs of their customers.

BENCHMARKING

Companies use benchmarking to identify the "Best Practices" of those companies that have gained recognition for their excellence in a particular area — such as Xerox for the development of human resources and Toyota for customer satisfaction. Benchmarking provides a systematic way to identify superior products, services, systems and processes that can be integrated and adapted into a company's current operations.

Benchmarking reveals what the best companies are measuring and indicates what the key factors are for world-class competition. Gains such as reduced costs, decreased cycle times and improved product quality are aimed at achieving greater precision in meeting internal and external customer requirements.

"Improvement is the organized creation of beneficial change, the attainment of unprecedented levels of performance."

J.M. Juran

186

Benchmarking includes profiling a company to learn how it achieved its improvements and the impact those improvements have had on the company's business practices and results in the marketplace. Companies gain insight into how another company redirected its way of doing things and what measurements it uses to assure continuous improvement.

Benchmarking provides an opportunity for a company to set attainable goals based on its competition. It also makes a company reflect on its own standards.

There are four general types of benchmarking: internal, competitive, world-class operations and activity type.

1. **Internal benchmarking** is when a company takes stock of the outputs of other departments, divisions and subsidiaries within its own company — a great, often overlooked source of innovation and improvement. This investigation should take place first to alert you to what resources exist internally, to attract support (financial and personal commitment) from colleagues in doing other types of benchmarking and to conserve your own financial resources for very select expenditures in other types of benchmarking. Internal benchmarking will focus your external benchmarking efforts in a more pragmatic way.

2. **Competitive benchmarking** involves the investigation of a competitor's products, services and processes. This is also known as "reverse engineering." Competitors' products are bought and disassembled and then compared for their design and assembly methods. Products are tested repeatedly to establish performance measures and all product literature is reviewed carefully. The goal is to determine greatest value for the least cost in the products as they respond best to customer requirements.

> *Benchmarking makes a company reflect on its own standards.*

187

3. **World-class operations benchmarking** extends the benchmarking process beyond a company's competitors and industry to identify companies who are excellent at doing specific things of significance to the investigating company. Many processes and systems are somewhat generic and have value for cross-over applications from one industry to another.

Xerox identified the following companies with whom they benchmarked for the corresponding purpose:

Organization	Purpose for Benchmarking
Canon	Photocopiers
DEC	Work stations
L.L. Bean	Warehouse operations
General Electric	Information systems
Deere	Service parts logistics
Ford	Assembly automation generic processes
Federal Reserve	Bill scanning
Citicorp	Document processing

4. **Activity type benchmarking** is directed at process steps or discreet activities such as order taking, reservations, accounts payable collections, recruiting, etc. This type of benchmarking cuts across dissimilar industries as well.

Benchmarking Checklist

The components that form the framework for benchmarking flow into six distinct phases: process design and planning, internal data collection, external data collection, data analysis, process upgrading and periodic reassessment. Companies committed to TQM know the value of utilizing this framework for benchmarking. They isolate and focus on particular phases and can make improvements in their own processes based on how they measure up.

The following are components of the benchmarking process:

- What will be benchmarked?
- What process will be compared?
- Which measurements will be used?
- Which internal areas and external companies will be benchmarked?
- How to collect and analyze the data?
- What accounts for the gap between your product and the "Best"?
- What action plans, targets and measurements are required for improvement?
- How to provide for updating the benchmarking process and evaluating its impact on improvements for the company?

Definitions

A unit of measurement (according to Juran) is a defined amount of some quality feature that permits evaluation of that feature in numbers. Examples include: time required to produce a product, cost per unit, number of employee suggestions during a given time and reduction in customer complaints.

Units of measure are developed for product deficiencies and for product features. The measurement for most product deficiencies is expressed by this commonly used formula:

$$\text{Quality} = \frac{\text{Frequency of deficiencies}}{\text{Opportunity for deficiencies}}$$

Frequency of deficiencies, the numerator, reflects such things as number of defects, number of errors, hours of rework, number of lost bids, dollar Cost of Poor Quality (COPQ) and change orders.

Opportunity for deficiencies, the denominator, takes such forms as total number of units produced, total project hours, total bid proposals, total operating budget and total project revenue.

The resulting units of measure appear as percent defective, percent errors, percent rework and COPQ per dollar of sales.

A **sensor** (as noted by Juran) is a method or instrument that can carry out the evaluation and state the findings in numbers in terms of a unit of measure. There are technological sensors, such as clocks, thermometers and various gauges. There are also human sensors that operate along a continuum of the hierarchy of measurement, such as decisions about how to classify results as they occur — analyzing, reporting and making recommendations to senior management. With both technological and human sensors, the two key concerns are accuracy and precision.

The **accuracy of the sensor** is the degree to which a sensor tells the truth — the extent to which its evaluations agree with the "true" value as judged by an agreed upon standard. The difference between the observed evaluations and the true value is the "error," which can be either positive or negative. It is usually easy to adjust technological sensors to achieve greater accuracy by recalibrating the instrument. It is less possible with human sensors, but nonetheless worthy of making an investment to train people and provide them with positive steps to attain credible sensing. (Note the chart on the facing page on Human Sensing Error Types and Remedies.)

The **precision of a sensor** is a measure of the ability of the sensor to reproduce its results on repeat tests. Technological sensors usually have a high reproducibility rate; yet precision at the higher ends will be limited by the design of the instrument. Human sensors are far less precise (inspectors, auditors, appraisers, supervisors). Keep human sensing to a minimum on critical quality features.

HUMAN SENSING ERROR TYPES AND REMEDIES

There are several common human sensing errors that occur in measurement. They are listed here along with the remedies that will keep them from occurring. When companies gain greater control over reducing errors, the quality improves, costs are reduced and customers have greater satisfaction.

Error Types	Remedies
Misinterpretation	Precise definition; glossary Checklists Examples
Inadvertent errors	Aptitude testing Reorganization of work to reduce fatigue and monotony Fail-safe designs Redundancy Foolproofing (errorproofing) Automation; robotics

Lack of technique	Discovery of knack of successful
	    workers
	Revision of technology to
	    incorporate the knack
	Retraining

Conscious errors	Design review of data-collection plan Removal of atmosphere of blame Action on reports, or explanation of why not Depersonalize the orders Establish accountability Provide balanced emphasis on goals Conduct quality audits Create competition, incentives Reassign work

> *"Self-generated quality control is more effective than inspector-generated quality control."*
>
> **Tom Peters**

191

CUSTOMER-DRIVEN MEASUREMENT PROCESS

A process to link business plans with customer requirements.

MARKET AND CUSTOMER REQUIREMENTS & ANALYSIS

↓

BUSINESS PLANS & STRATEGIES

↓

Goal
is to
link
the
process

FUNCTIONAL OBJECTIVES & MEASUREMENTS

↓

DEPARTMENTAL OBJECTIVES & MEASUREMENTS

↓

INDIVIDUAL AND TEAM OBJECTIVES & MEASUREMENTS

SAMPLE BUSINESS PLANNING MODEL

The Customer-Driven Measurement Process guides business planning. To utilize the Business Planning Model on the worksheet that starts on page 195, review this sample outline and then complete the Business Planning Worksheet for your department.

Overall Strategies

1   Introduce new products ahead of the competition based on market and customer requirements

2   Defend existing products (market share, profit margins)

3   Increase product quality

Functional Objectives

1   **R & D**
    — Identify next generation technology by "X" date.

2   **Manufacturing**
    — Increase market share on product line "X" by producing 15.9 million in the next fiscal year.

3   **Quality**
    — Improve quality-data collecting, retrieval and analysis systems for all product lines by "X" date.

4   **Customer Support**
    — Improve overall customer support and field service response times for problem-solving and repair service by "X" date.

5   **Software Engineering**
    — Improve software forecasting ability for new product "X" by the beginning of the next fiscal year.

> *"Challenging/ rethinking our boundaries — in other words FRAMEBRAKING."*
>
> *Jack Welsh*

6 **Finance**
   — Provide financial-analysis tools and turnaround
   reports on a timely basis (week, month, quarter)
   to support smooth operation of the business.

7 **Sales**
   — Increase sales for product "X" by 15% and market
   share by 8% during the next fiscal year.

Customer-Driven Measurement Process

The Customer-Driven Measurement Process demonstrates how
customer requirements drive business plans and strategies that
dictate functional, departmental and individual objectives and
measurements. Evaluation of all the measurements relates back
to satisfaction of customer requirements.

Product and process improvements depend on a high-quality,
integrated system of measurement that provides timely and
responsive communication loops with customers and suppliers
on a routine basis. This integrated measurement process
provides the clearest path to continuous improvement. The
concept is reflected in the "Checklist for Measurements" and
"Activities That Affect Costs in a Quality System" to be
introduced later.

Exercise

Review the steps of the Customer-Driven Measurement Process
on the diagram and note the influence the customer has on the
entire process. After you review the Customer-Driven
Measurement Process, review the Sample Business Planning
outline and see how functional goals reflect business strategies.

Now, develop your own objectives as a manager or supervisor
using the Business Planning Worksheet on the facing page to
work through some logical key objectives for departments,
teams and yourself. Include a measurement mechanism to
determine how effective the results will be in meeting
objectives. (You might find the exercise at the end of this
chapter on "Improving Team Effectiveness — Output and
Measurement" to be useful here. If you prefer, you can do the
exercise with the assigned role of Director of R&D and use the

Exercise

Sample Business Planning Model and the worksheet to
develop objectives and measurements for departments, teams
and yourself to achieve the stated functional objectives.)

Objectives need to specify a measurable goal toward which
your efforts and those of the group (company, division,
department or team) are organized. Verifiable objectives
facilitate measurement of the effectiveness and efficiency of
managerial actions and group effort.

BUSINESS PLANNING WORKSHEET

What are the components of your overall business strategy?

1. _____

2. _____

3. _____

1. Identify key functional objective(s) and a measurement for each.

Objective	Measurement
_____	_____
_____	_____
_____	_____

2. Identify key departmental/team objective(s) and a measurement
for each.

Objective	Measurement
_____	_____
_____	_____
_____	_____

BUSINESS PLANNING WORKSHEET (continued)

3. Identify key objective(s) and a measurement for the output of
   employees whose work you direct.

Objective	Measurement
_____	_____
_____	_____
_____	_____

4. Identify your key objective(s) as a manager or supervisor and a
   measurement for each.

Objective	Measurement
_____	_____
_____	_____
_____	_____

WHAT THINGS GET MEASURED AND WHEN

Companies need to make measurement a key component in their continuous-improvement process. There are several ways to approach an understanding of what things get measured in a company; one perspective states simply that anything worth doing is worth measuring. This attitude drives companies to measure everything and discover which efforts either add value or detract value in producing their products and services according to the requirements of their customers. This comprehensive attack is guaranteed to drive costs down. Begin with your customers' latest complaints!

As noted previously, measurements are designed to assess major business processes including financial indicators, product and process quality, and quality and quality improvements. The data that is collected, recorded and analyzed informs the company about:

1. **Ongoing Results** — The company needs a "real-time" log of day-to-day activities and results that meet production schedules, respond to customer demands or contribute value to general operations. Some examples are response times, on-time deliveries, reduction in customer complaints and growth in market share.

2. **Process/Product Improvements** — Reports identifying progress being made with specific initiatives related to improvements in product development and upgrades, work process flow and customer service are essential to keep management and all contributors (customers, employees, suppliers) up-to-date. Improvements are a tonic for everyone and reinforce commitment. Some examples are successful new product introduction related to customer input during planning and improved distribution system, and decreased cycle time related to improvements in software engineering.

Anything worth doing is worth measuring.

197

3. **Quality and Quality Improvements** — The ability to determine the impact of the quality process and expenditures for quality improvements is important to demonstrate value being delivered in cost savings to the customer and increased sales and growth in market share for the company. Demonstrating "savings" to a company for controlling the Cost of Poor Quality (COPQ) — discussed under "Quality Cost Techniques" — reminds the company that the investment in quality pays off.

Measurements are done at three intervals in tracking any process: before, during and after delivery. Repeat measurement is key in discovering your progress toward goals and the performance reliability (precision) of what is being measured. Performance over time is essential to understand a capability and its capacity for impacting results.

Who Is Responsible for Measurements?

The person closest to the process being measured should be the one responsible for measuring, keeping records and providing feedback to others. You will be this person sometimes. Then, you should contribute your interpretation and analysis and make suggestions related to potential strategies for improvements. Cross-functional problem-solving and improvement teams working in TQM environments take this responsibility seriously and know the importance of feeding back results to their companies.

Companies must commit to training people in designing and implementing measurement systems. People need to learn what to measure, how to measure, which tools to use, how to develop documentation and how to explore the impact and use of the data they observe and record. People throughout the company need to become active in measuring and accountable for reporting and analyzing data and making recommendations. You are beginning your training through this manual.

Checklist for Measurements

Review the Checklist for Measurements below to see how measurements serve the goal of highest quality for "Best Cost" for the customer. The checklist demonstrates what some companies think is important to measure and how they categorize and cluster different factors. This checklist was compiled from the measures of priority items of respective companies as indicated after each category; obviously, no single company's entire list of measurements is represented. Notice how the measurements are organized and brainstorm your own company's approach to measurements.

Check with an "X" the measurements that you or your company already maintain, and mark the ones you need to develop with an "N" under "Status." Also note when you conduct the measurement for each item — before (B), during (D), and/or after (A) delivery to the customer.

CHECKLIST FOR MEASUREMENTS

Measurement	Status (X,N)	When (B,D,A)
KEY OPERATING INDICATORS (*Florida Power & Light*)		
Operating and maintenance cost per customer	___	___
Customers per employee	___	___
Operating and maintenance cost— % change vs. consumer price index	___	___
Customer/employee improvement index	___	___
Credit memos per 1,000 customers	___	___
Extension costs per new service account	___	___
Public Service inquiries per 1,000 customers	___	___
Average hours vehicle utilization	___	___
Service unavailability index	___	___
Service interruptions per 100 miles	___	___

CHECKLIST FOR MEASUREMENTS (continued)

QUALITY MEASURES
(Westinghouse Nuclear Fuels Div.)
Customer satisfaction
Fuel reliability
Software errors
Software delivery
Fuel assembly yield
Tubeshield yield
Cladding yield
Total quality costs

CUSTOMER FEEDBACK
(Texas Instruments-TI)
Returns due to electrical, mechanical
    and visual problems
Returns due to administrative errors
Unjustified returns
Product quality & reliability
TI's ranking on quality & reliability vs.
    the competition
TI's quality of service

COST OF QUALITY
(Texas Instruments)
Cost of conformance
Cost of nonconformance
Total cost of quality
Total cost of quality as a percentage of
    total manufacturing cost

QUALITY COST TECHNIQUES

Quality cost techniques provide a tool for the management of a company to "fine-tune" the quality system. All departments of a company are occupied with measurements in the quality system: marketing, product design, manufacturing, accounting, service and others. Suppliers are equal partners in being accountable for measuring quality costs and committing to improvements.

The case has been made already that meeting customer requirements is the No. 1 factor in determining the quality of a company and its products and services. Precision in the quality system is imperative. Quality cost techniques provide a systematic way of measuring, reporting and tracking the effectiveness and efficiency of all parts in the system working together at various junctures in the process.

Input → Throughput → Output → Phases

The four major cost categories within the quality system are:

1. Prevention   (Input Phase)

2. Appraisal   (Input Phase)

3. Internal Failure (Throughput Phase)

4. External Failure (Output Phase)

Although quality costs may average over one-third of product costs, the greatest expenditure is for failures — 20% of product costs. The implications are clear in how much more companies must focus on listening to the customer to clarify customer requirements at the beginning of a project. More time and enhanced expertise is required during the planning stage.

Quality cost techniques provide you and management with a way of assessing relationships between money expended for a certain activity on both a micro-departmental and a macro-divisional level. Relationships among departments and those within departments can be evaluated. Tracking quality costs is important to supplement the accounting system to demonstrate effort spent on activities in the quality system. Recording expenditures in terms of dollars provides a systems approach to improving quality. Recommendations for changes can be

> *"Quality is so important it pays for itself."*
>
> *Andrew J. DuBrin*

201

*$'s
and
Sense*

made to improve preventive efforts that will result in greater customer satisfaction, which leads to increased sales and improved profit margins.

ACTIVITIES THAT AFFECT COSTS IN A QUALITY SYSTEM

The following demonstrates typical activities performed by various departments that affect costs within a quality system. Note where you are incurring costs in your own quality system with an "X" in the status column and whether or not ("Y" or "N") you are measuring results for that expenditure. Expenditures are grouped under the four major cost categories in a quality system — prevention, appraisal, internal failure and external failure.

PREVENTION COSTS		Status	Y/N
Marketing	Marketing research	____	____
	Customer-perception surveys	____	____
	Customer-satisfaction surveys	____	____
	Contract review	____	____
Product Design & Development	Quality progress reviews	____	____
	Support activities	____	____
	Qualification tests	____	____
	Field trials	____	____
Purchasing	Supplier reviews	____	____
	Supplier rating	____	____
	PO technical data reviews	____	____
	Supplier quality planning	____	____
Operations	Process validation	____	____
	Operations quality planning	____	____
	Operations support quality planning	____	____
	Operator quality education	____	____
	Operator Statistical Process Control	____	____
	Design & development	____	____
	Quality-related equipment	____	____

PREVENTION COSTS (continued)		Status	Y/N
Quality Administration	Administrative salaries	___	___
	Administrative expenses	___	___
	Quality program planning	___	___
	Quality performance reporting	___	___
	Quality education	___	___
	Quality improvement	___	___
	Quality audits	___	
APPRAISAL COSTS		Status	Y/N
Purchasing	Receiving inspection/tests	___	___
	Inspection equipment	___	___
	Supplier product qualification	___	___
	Vendor-certification process	___	___
Operations	Performance of planned test/audits	___	___
	— labor	___	___
	— quality audits	___	___
	— inspection & test materials	___	___
	Manufacturing tests	___	___
	Process-control measurements	___	___
	Laboratory support	___	___
	Inspection & test equipment	___	___
	Certification by external groups	___	___
External	Field performance evaluation	___	___
	Special product evaluation	___	___
	Field stock & spare parts evaluation	___	___
	Test and inspection data review	___	___

203

INTERNAL FAILURE COSTS		Status	Y/N
Product Design	Corrective action	___	___
	Rework — design changes	___	___
	Scrap — design changes	___	___
	Production liaison costs	___	___
Purchasing	Purchased material reject costs	___	___
	Purchased material replacement costs	___	___
	Supplier corrective action	___	___
	Rework of supplier rejects	___	___
	Uncontrolled material losses	___	___
Operations	Failure analysis	___	___
	Investigation report	___	___
	Corrective action	___	___
	Rework/repair	___	___
	Reinspection	___	___
	Scrap	___	___
	Downgraded end product	___	___
	Labor losses	___	___

EXTERNAL FAILURE COSTS	Status	Y/N
Customer complaint investigation and resolution	_____	_____
Returned goods evaluation		
— repair	_____	_____
— replace	_____	_____
Retrofit costs	_____	_____
Recall costs	_____	_____
Warranty costs	_____	_____
Liability costs	_____	_____
Penalties	_____	_____
Customer goodwill	_____	_____
Lost sales	_____	_____

IMPROVING TEAM EFFECTIVENESS — OUTPUT AND MEASUREMENT

One of the most important responsibilities of a manager or supervisor is to balance individual goals with the synergy a team can develop. The productivity of your team needs to focus on the functional and departmental objectives that have been established to reflect business strategies. Your team needs to establish its own objectives and measurements with the goal of improving work process and increasing customer satisfaction.

One of the methods for establishing team effectiveness is to facilitate a Team Analysis of Current Work (facing page). Each member of your team participates in a group analysis of how the department or the team is performing. A series of meetings may be necessary and people may need to spend some time outside the meeting gathering data related to the results of their work.

A Force Field Analysis might be useful to determine positive and restraining forces that affect team functioning and output. A cause-and-effect diagram is another tool to facilitate discussion and analysis of the effectiveness of your team's work process. The goal of this analysis is to streamline workflow, focus jobs and create a sense of ownership in making improvements.

Examine the Team Analysis of Current Work to see how customer requirements drive business strategy and direct the formation of objectives throughout the company. As your team troubleshoots its own process, you will discover areas for improvements. The worksheet for Improving the Team's Output on page 208 will be useful to you as you process your analysis.

SYNERGISM n.
the simultaneous action of separate agencies which, together, have greater total effect than the sum of their individual effects.

Webster's

206

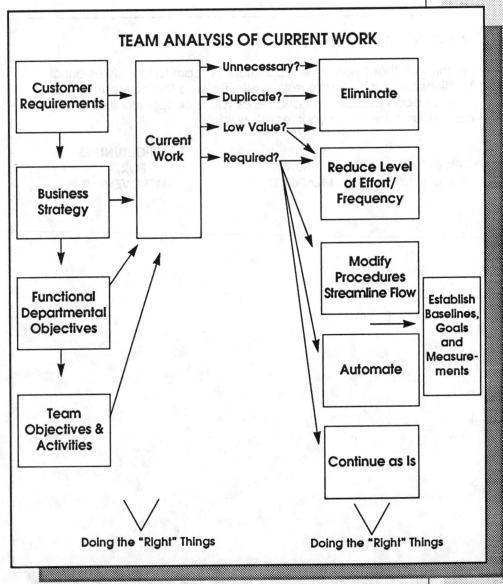

TEAM ANALYSIS OF CURRENT WORK

Customer Requirements

Business Strategy

Functional Departmental Objectives

Team Objectives & Activities

Current Work

Unnecessary?
Duplicate? → Eliminate
Low Value?
Required?

Reduce Level of Effort/ Frequency

Modify Procedures Streamline Flow

Establish Baselines, Goals and Measure- ments

Automate

Continue as Is

Doing the "Right" Things

Doing the "Right" Things

207

IMPROVING THE TEAM'S OUTPUT

Use this worksheet with your department or team to identify essential functions for which you are responsible. Refer to the diagram on the previous page to assist your analysis as you seek opportunities to improve and streamline your team's output.

ESSENTIAL FUNCTIONS	HOW MEASURED?	OPPORTUNITIES FOR IMPROVEMENT
1.		
2.		
3.		
4.		
5.		

CHAPTER 12

Four Programs

INTRODUCTION

The successful integration of people and technology improves
overall quality within an organization. Chapter 9 examined
strategies aimed at improving an employee's knowledge, skills
and abilities. This chapter discusses three programs, all of
which aim to improve work processes and focus on the
technology aspect of TQM.

The programs examined — Socio-Technical Systems (STS),
Statistical Process Control (SPC), Just-in-Time (JIT) inventory
control and International Organization for Standardization
(ISO) 9000 — are some of the primary TQM programs
currently used by organizations throughout the world. This
chapter will provide you with a basic understanding of each
program.

> *The successful
> integration of
> people and
> technology
> improves overall
> quality within an
> organization.*

SOCIO-TECHNICAL SYSTEMS (STS)

The concept of Socio-Technical Systems is based on the work of Eric Trist, who studied the ways technology was introduced in British coal mines. He found that when workers were allowed to participate in the design of the changes, productivity increased. This situation illustrated how the human system must interact with the technical system to ensure smooth integration. His work has been advanced by several companies, with the goal of creating an organization that can rapidly adapt to changing external and internal environments.

Program Aim

- Determine how well the social and technical systems are designed with respect to one another and with respect to the demands of the external environment improve where necessary.

- Evaluate/develop an organizational structure that functions as an open system.

Terminology

- **Social System** — Employee interpersonal systems (communication system)

- **Technical System** — How technology is applied to the worksite (computer system)

- **Open System** — An open system evaluates performance against standards that are themselves subject to evaluation (views organizations as able to learn)

Five factors are required for a successful STS program.

1. **Examine each system as part of the larger organization.**

   — No work process is seen as isolated from the larger process.

2. **Program must be built on principles.**

   — Program leaders are responsible for defining the principles in addition to clearly communicating the company's vision to all employees.

3. **The STS intervention should not dictate improvements.** Instead, all employees directly affected should participate in the improvement of the work processes involved. Quality results from commitment and teamwork.

4. **All work should be designed to be value adding.** Each person's actions must add value to those of other employees. Redundancy of functions should be eliminated.

5. **Program should not be designed to be "good enough."** The intervention should look beyond the status quo and toward "ideal" solutions.

> *Factors for successful STS Program.*

IMPROVING TECHNICAL SYSTEMS

Technical systems include, among others, transportation, data capturing and work station systems.

Q: How can one analyze and redesign work processes?

A: There is no one right way to analyze and redesign a work process.

The following steps have, however, proved successful in many companies.

1. Identify key processes
2. Gather data
3. Define the current situation
4. Define the ideal situation
5. Pilot test the ideal situation
6. Complete a cost-benefit analysis
7. Present findings to management/decision makers

FLOW DIAGRAMS

One of the first steps to improve a process is to identify the sequential activities that are necessary to complete the process. The flow diagram is a pictorial view of the process that shows each activity, using various symbols to identify each step as follows:

Start → Activity → Decision → Delay → End

The flow diagram is an essential tool for improving the socio-technical system by mapping the workflow and work process with the involvement of the workers. As mentioned earlier, this is a critical method of introducing technology, eliminating waste/non-value-added activities and continuously improving processes. The key element is to involve the work unit in the analysis and decision-making stages. This typically occurs by brainstorming a flow diagram as a group. The result is a picture of how the process is done today. In the analysis and decision-making stages, the group decides how to streamline the process to make it more efficient. In some cases, jobs may change as some tasks are combined. This usually is a positive process because of the involvement of the employees.

Flow diagrams are valuable not only for teams but also for individuals to see how to improve their work processes.

212

FLOW DIAGRAM

Examples

Start of Activity

Phone rings — ○ — ❑ — ■ — ◊ — ○   **End**

| | Answer the Phone | Confirm understanding of customer's comments | Decide to refer to Customer Service Manager | Transfer Call | **of Activity** |

Start of Activity

Phone rings — ❑ — ■ — ❑ — ❑ — **End**

| | Answer the Phone | Confirm under-standing | Record customer's comments | Salutation Put down phone | **of Activity** |

Practice Exercise: Consider a work process with which you are familiar. Using the symbols explained above, develop a flow diagram to represent the activity.

213

SPC is a method of establishing control limits for a process and to respond to variations that exceed the control limits.

STATISTICAL PROCESS CONTROL (SPC)

SPC is a method of establishing control limits for a process and to respond to variations that exceed the control limits. The goals of SPS include:

- Conformance to specification
- Removal of unacceptable variation
- Control of a process within established tolerances

Program Aim

- Improve quality of products/services
- Take measurements to determine whether quality of products/services falls within preset parameters
- Chart measurements to show trends (variations from set standards)

Premises of SPC Design

1. Program can be used in both a service and production environment.

2. Work "outputs" must be recorded graphically (data can be presented using, among others, flow charts, control charts and scatter diagrams).

3. Once trends are identified, one of two things can occur:

   — The standards of performance (quality parameters) can be made more stringent.

   — Adjustments/corrective action can be made to the work process.

   Note: TQM principles emphasize the importance of using customer requirements as the standard against which the quality of work is measured.

Suggestions for Applying SPC to Your Company

Begin with an area within your organization where definite improvements can be made. An example: customer inquiries take too long to resolve.

Begin with and chart an area within your organization that is important to the success of a specific department.

Begin recording data as early as possible in the sequence of tasks that make up the process. For instance, chart the number of phone calls answered per hour within a customer service department before charting the number of customer complaints filed each day.

Begin charting a process that is easily measured. Measurements yielded should be reliable (consistently available over time) and valid (meaningful to the total process).

Statistical Terms

1. Mean/Average — represented by the symbol $\overline{X}$ (X bar)

    Example 1: Customer service department answers 30 calls on Monday, 15 on Tuesday, 25 on Wednesday, 12 on Thursday and 18 on Friday.

    $$\overline{X} = \frac{30 + 15 + 25 + 12 + 18}{5}$$

    $$\overline{X} = 20$$

2. Range (symbol R) is the difference between the highest and lowest of a sample or group of numbers.

    Example 2: Using the same numbers as in Example 1:
    Range = 30 - 18 = 12

    (Note: If you are using negative numbers, ignore the sign; when calculating the range, view all numbers as positive.)

> "The longest journey is the journey inwards of him who has chosen his destiny."
>
> **Dag Hammarskjöld**

Example

215

3. Variation/Sigma/Standard Deviation represented by the symbol σ (sigma). Sigma represents how close all your measurements are to the average.

Sigma is a useful statistic in that it determines how confident you can be if you use the mean to represent all measurements. Therefore, the closer sigma is to the mean, the greater your confidence can be in using the mean to describe the data.

(Note: When all the measurements equal the average, sigma is equal to zero.)

The larger your sigma value, the more spread out your measurements are from each other and the mean.

$$\sigma = \frac{\bar{R}}{d^2}$$

$\bar{R}$ = The average range
d^2 is obtained from a statistical table

Sample	d^2
2	1.128
3	1.693
4	2.059
5	2.326

(table continues)

Example 3: You have calculated three ranges, namely, 8, 6 and 10 from a sample of five numbers.

$$\bar{R} = \frac{8 + 6 + 10}{3}$$

$$R = 8$$

$$\sigma = \frac{8}{2.326}$$

σ = 3.44 (rounded off to two decimal places)

216

Check Your Understanding

Q1: Using the following data, calculate the average and the range.

10, 12, 16, 19 + 27

Average _____ Range _____

Q2: You take four measurements during a day. You calculate the average of all ranges to be 5.5.

What is your sample size?

What is the d^2 we use?

Calculate σ (sigma):

Answers:

Q1: Average = 16.8 Range = 17

Q2: Sample size = 4 (four measurements)

d^2 = 2.059 (from previous table)

$$\sigma = \frac{5.5}{2.059}$$

σ = 2.67 (rounded off to two decimal places)

Two additional statistical terms are required to construct a control chart, namely, upper and lower control limits.

Upper Control Limit = UCL $\overline{X} = X + A_2 \overline{R}$

$\overline{X}$ = grand average and is the average of all our averages.

(A_2 = is obtained from a table and is determined by the size of the subgroup being charted.)

217

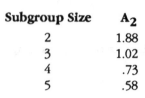

Subgroup Size	A_2
2	1.88
3	1.02
4	.73
5	.58

$\bar{R}$ = average of the ranges

UCL = represents an area "above" the mean value in which 49.35% of our X values should fall when plotted. Any values outside this area indicate something unusual in your process.

Example 4: If $\bar{X}$ = 10

   Subgroup sample size = 4

   $\bar{R}$ = 3

   UCL $\bar{X}$ = $\bar{X} + A_2 \ \bar{R}$

                    = 10 + .73 multiplied by 3

                    = 10 + 2.19

                    = 12.19

Lower Control Limit = LCL $\overline{X}$ = $\overline{X}$ - A$_2$ $\overline{R}$

LCL $\overline{X}$ = represents an area "below" the mean value in which the remaining 49.35% of our values should fall when plotted. Any values outside this area indicate something unusual in your process.

Example 5: Use the same figures as in Example 4.

LCL $\overline{X}$ = $\overline{X}$ - A$_2$ $\overline{R}$

= 10 - (.73) multiplied by 3

= 10 - 2.19

= 7.81

Example

Constructing a Control Chart

By using the values calculated from Examples 4 and 5, you can construct the following control chart.

Plot points that fall above the UCL can indicate an unusual process (out of control).

UCL $\overline{X}$
12.19

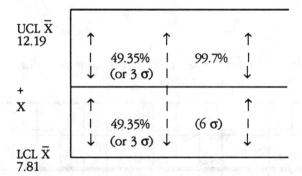

+
$\overline{X}$

LCL $\overline{X}$
7.81

Plot points that fall within the UCL and LCL indicate a normal process.

Plot points that fall below the LCL can indicate an unusual process (out of control).

$\overline{X}$ is usually drawn as a solid dark line.
UCL and LCL are usually drawn as dotted lines.

"When you can measure what you are speaking about, and express it in numbers, you know something about it ... "

Lord Kelvin
William Thomson

Determinants of Out-of-Control Process

A control chart is constructed to plot measurements recorded while observing a work process.

The aim is to determine whether the process is in or out of control.

The following charts indicate that your work process is probably out of control.

Shift

A shift is seven plot points in a row that all fall either above or below the center line (X), indicating an unusual process.

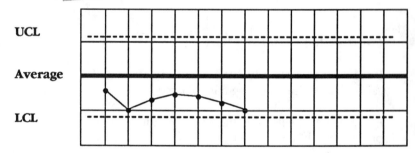

Trend

A trend is six or more consecutive plot points going up or down from any one anchor point.

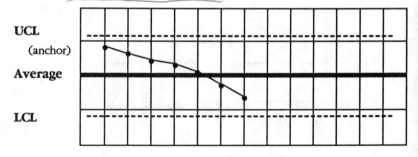

Jump

A jump is a change of more than 4 σ between two plot points. (Remember that the distance from the center line (X) to either the UCL or LCL is 3 σ.)

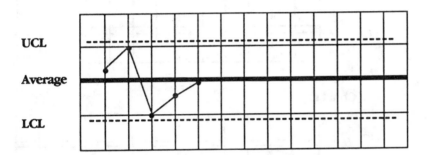

Shifts, trends and jumps often occur after a change has been made, such as new equipment installed or employees trained. Plotting the observations enables you to tell whether the change(s) had a positive or negative effect on the process.

Before taking any corrective action, you should identify the reason(s) behind the changes observed.

Check Your Understanding

Examine the control charts below. Which chart shows a process that is in statistical control?

Chart A

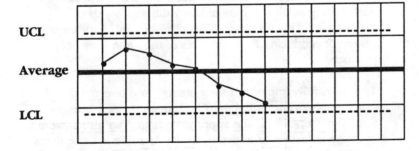

221

Chart B

UCL

Average

LCL

Chart C

UCL

Average

LCL

Chart B is in statistical control. (Note: This does not necessarily mean that you should leave the process alone. There may be opportunities to improve the process and obtain substantial benefits.)

JUST-IN-TIME PROGRAM (JIT)

Taiichi Ohno, the man who pioneered Just-in-Time at Toyota, developed this concept out of a need to provide a system to manufacture small numbers of many different kinds of automobiles. This was very different from the U.S. production system of producing large amounts of the same kind of products.

To successfully implement his system, Ohno directed that the exact number of required units be brought to each successive stage of production at the appropriate time. The results were a dramatic reduction of inventory and a decrease in cycle times. It is this foundation that provides the basis for application of JIT techniques that go beyond the traditional production settings.

JIT or Just in Time — productivity and quality are inseparable and therefore shape the inventory demand.

Program Aim

- Produce to exact demand
- Continuous improvement
- Eliminate waste

Premises of JIT Design

1. People are the source of quality and productivity.
2. JIT is not dependent on the culture of your workforce.
3. Traditional management believes that practices need to be changed.
4. Cutting inventories is not the only way to eliminate waste.

A JIT program has many components. The key components featured here are improvement teams, vendor relations and quality at the source.

Organizations use the following components:

"The goal of a JIT system is 100% good items at each manufacturing step."

Andrew J. DuBrin

Customer Demands and Requirements

→

Your Organization Demands "X" from Vendors

- **Improvement Teams**
- **Control over Vendor Relations**
- **Quality-at-the-Source Approach**

→ **Customer Expectations Met**

JIT — Improvement Teams

Improvement teams are a means to implement JIT principles. An excellent opportunity exists to make use of the team concept outlined in Chapter 9. As a vehicle to support JIT, the improvement team can focus on specific approaches to meeting demand forecasts and eliminating waste while achieving incremental improvements.

223

Program Aim:

Improve the Organization

- Meet and exceed customer requirements
- Utilize new ideas and techniques
- Improve the quality of supplies received

Build a Better Workplace

- Trust employees
- Utilize their knowledge
- Develop human resources

Develop Individual Knowledge, Skills and Abilities

- Supervisors
- Team leaders
- Latent abilities of employees

Focus Can Be on:

- Safety improvements (Example: OSHA compliance team)

- Productivity/efficiency improvements (Example: Saturn Motor Division's manufacturing team)

- Quality improvements (Example: Training department and trainee team review training materials)

- Morale improvements (Example: Establish a recognition and rewards team)

JIT — Vendor Relations

Program Aim:

To establish long-term partnerships with single-source suppliers. Suppliers must be committed to providing the highest-quality materials/service while continuously reducing costs. This will ensure the continued opportunity to conduct business and become a sole-source supplier.

JIT is best used in a repetitive, single-product manufacturing environment.

Traditional vs. JIT Approach to Purchasing Services or Goods

Place a check mark next to the relationship which best describes your organization.

Traditional	JIT Approach
• Annual contract	• Long-term relationship
• Paper overload	• Reduced paperwork
• Competing bids	• Negotiate price based upon cost analysis
• Receiver inspects goods/services	• Supplier checks and certifies quality
• Each part/service may have multiple sources	• Single sourcing for a group of parts or services

The JIT approach to vendor relations creates a new role for purchasing agents/buyers. The skills of these employees must be developed, with emphasis on negotiation, cooperative relations and long-term planning.

Buyers must now manage the suppliers' networks and negotiate price reductions. In addition, the quality of goods/services must be guaranteed/warranted by suppliers.

JIT — Quality at the Source

Program Aim:

Each operation must view the next operation as its customer. Each department must view the other departments as its customer. Therefore, each operation/department must do it right the first time. You and your team must do it right the first time.

You and your team must do it right the first time.

225

The driving force behind quality at the source is that each worker should be responsible for quality. This translates into no quality-control inspections and trusting workers' judgments.

If something does go wrong, stop process immediately and check for:

- Defective parts/equipment
- Overproduction (waste)
- Safety hazards

Quality at the source may be the single most important TQM concept. If each employee takes responsibility for doing things right the first time, every day, at every level, the quality and reliability of the company will immediately be recognized. When this is combined with effective leadership — providing direction on the right tasks — the results are very powerful.

Key JIT Components at Work

JIT concepts and applications are most often associated with manufacturing operations. The following example is cited to give you a sense of how JIT works outside a production setting.

Example: Applying JIT components within a human resources department.

Task: Fill a vacant position in engineering.

Title: Engineering Manager

Step 1: HR department in consultation with engineering department sets date by which position will be filled with most qualified applicant.

Assumption:

— 60 days set as time frame
— Organization uses several placement companies

Step 2: In consultation, HR department and engineering department choose one vendor. Vendor should be chosen on the basis of reputation for quality, not lowest cost.

Clearly explain requirements and negotiate cost for service.

Assumption:

If vendor provides quality service, you will establish a long-term partnership with this company.

Step 3: Trust vendor to screen applicants. Trust vendor to send *only* candidates who meet and exceed minimum qualifications.

Step 4: Any candidates should be interviewed by a team comprising both HR and engineering staff.

Team should jointly determine the structure of the interview and the criteria against which all applicants will be measured.

Assumption:

No second interview of candidates will be required. Do it right the first time.

Step 5: Choose candidate within the 60-day time period.

Step 6: Negotiate a long-term contract with vendor. Negotiate a "volume discount."

Assumption:

Vendor's performance met or exceeded your requirements.

Example

Final Note: If the vendor failed to begin sending qualified applicants within, for example, 10 days, stop the process and renegotiate with vendor. Should the vendor continue not to send qualified applicants in the next seven days, sever the relationship. HR and engineering would then reassess other vendors if none is found suitable. Alternative placements should be considered. The 60-day time frame should not be changed since total quality is your aim.

Suggestions for Applying JIT to Your Company

The JIT concept has many benefits. Unfortunately, it has become another "buzzword." One method of showing the positive aspects of JIT is to begin a pilot program. The pilot test has become an excellent vehicle for transferring technology by demonstrating results through a committed group of employees and managers. The idea behind the pilot is to "load it for success."

Preparation

1. Pilot test in one specific department in your organization.
2. Pick an area with the most motivated people.
3. Understand the premises of JIT.
4. Make continuous small improvements your goal.
5. Develop a plan of action for your pilot JIT program.

Your Pilot JIT Program Should Include the Following Enabling Factors

1. **Strong leadership from top management**
   - Clearly seen to be committed
   - Possess an understanding of JIT principles
   - Assist in the selection of the steering committee
   - Gain union support and representation

2. **Select a steering committee**
   - Appoint a project leader (who will work full time as the liaison between the pilot area and management)
   - Provide resources
   - Conduct periodic reviews
   - Include employees from the pilot area

3. **Conduct briefings**
   - For management, steering committee and project team
   - Management and teams should have ready access to JIT material/publications/videos, etc.

4. **Pilot planning**
   - Establish improvement goals
   - Review and "measure" current operations
   - Set target schedule

5. **Sell to employees (in pilot area)**
   - Get management approval
   - Conduct employee briefings
   - Explain team participation
   - Present cost/benefit analysis

6. **Employee training**
   - All affected workers
   - Check for employee understanding
   - Answer employee concerns
   - Review pilot plan (may need to be modified)

7. **Pilot implementation**
   - Record observations
   - Ensure feedback of results to (a) employees, (b) steering committee, (c) project team and (d) management
   - Revise strategy as needed
   - Publish positive gains observed (newsletter, etc.)

8. **Debriefing after pilot implementation**
   - Record findings in writing
   - Note problems encountered and lessons learned
   - Document benefits
   - Make a formal presentation

9. **Extend to a second area**
   - Select new project
   - Identify new project leaders and team members
   - Consider running parallel implementation strategies

INTERNATIONAL ORGANIZATION FOR STANDARDIZATION

ISO 9000

The International Organization for Standardization (ISO) was established in 1947 with the long-term goal of improving international understanding, communication and cooperation with respect to commerce and trade growth. The ISO has been able to foster several technical agreements that have been accepted as international standards.

The ISO is headquartered in Geneva, Switzerland, and has emerged as the international agency for standardization. Its members are composed of the decision makers from more than 90 countries that represent more than 90% of worldwide industrial output.

In 1987 the ISO made public a series of international standards that helped to clarify and define quality assurance. Those standards are defined in the ISO documents 9000, 9001, 9002, 9003 and 9004, on the following pages.

The European Community (EC) has adopted the ISO 9000 standards and will soon require companies selling products in Europe to comply with these standards, as certified by a third party. The implications for companies doing business on a global scale are enormous. Complying with ISO 9000 standards is becoming a strategic advantage for companies that have already taken the initiative to achieve certification.

ISO 9000 — quality standards accepted and supported by international businesses.

The ISO 9000 is based on the premise that:

- A quality production and management system will assure the desired level of quality

- An external assessment conducted by a third party will provide the most effective method of certification

ISO 9000 STANDARDS

ISO 9000   Establishes guidelines on the selection and use of quality management and quality assurance standards.

Key Questions

1. Does my company have an overall quality policy that has been endorsed by top management?

2. Does my company provide overall management of quality by including quality in strategic plans? By allocating resources to assure that quality standards are met?

3. Does my company's operational tools, techniques and programs ensure quality control and conformance to specifications?

4. Do I have the ability to audit ongoing operations to ensure adherence to quality standards?

231

ISO 9001 Establishes model for quality assurance in design/development, production, installation and servicing.

Key Questions

1. Does my company conduct regular product-design reviews to verify conformance to specifications?

2. Does my company have a responsive organization in place that can identify nonconformance problems and implement solutions on a timely basis?

3. Does my company collect and maintain documentation to validate products and processes?

4. Does my company provide in-process inspection and testing? Final inspection and testing? Are records current and readily available?

ISO 9002 Establishes a model quality assurance in production and installation.

Key Questions

1. Can my company trace all products during all stages of production and installation?

2. Does my company have documented work instructions to clearly define the manner of production and installation?

3. Do criteria exist to establish quality workmanship?

4. Do operations areas have documented procedures for handling, storage, packaging and delivery of products?

ISO 9003   Establishes a model for final inspection and test.

Key Questions

1. Can my company ensure calibration of key measuring devices?

2. Does my company have documented procedures on handling repaired or reworked products?

3. Are my employees trained in all aspects of testing? Is training documented?

ISO 9004   Establishes guidelines on the elements of quality management and quality systems.

Key Questions

1. Does my company adhere to a "quality loop" that examines all phases from initial identification to final satisfaction of requirements with respect to:

   a. Marketing and market research?
   b. Design/specification engineering and product development?
   c. Procurement?
   d. Process planning and development?
   e. Production?
   f. Inspection, testing and examination?
   g. Packaging and storage?
   h. Sales and distribution?
   i. Installation and operation?
   j. Technical assistance and maintenance?
   k. Disposal after use?

2. Are my company's operational procedures designed to facilitate continuous control and rapid response to required corrective actions?

3. Does my company provide field support for new or redesigned products?

233

Next Steps to Acquire ISO 9000 Certification

Meeting the ISO 9000 criteria is becoming a competitive advantage for companies who have committed to ISO 9000 as a business strategy. Here are some key steps you should consider in moving toward certification. This list will also serve as a preliminary checklist in getting started.

Step	Date Completed
1. Enlist the support of your quality assurance or quality control manager.	
2. Prepare a presentation for your senior management team that explains the ISO 9000 certification process. This should include advantages, benefits and costs for registration.	
3. Secure a copy of the complete set of ISO 9000 standards.	
4. Form an improvement team whose goal is to identify what needs to be done, in project planning format.	
5. Conduct a review/audit of your existing procedures as compared with the ISO 9000 standards.	
6. Complete a gap analysis and prepare plans to make necessary improvements.	
7. Contact a consultant or third party to help assess your audit and to advise your company on specific improvements.	
8. Revise and update all systems, procedures and manuals to reflect compliance to standards.	

Meeting the ISO 9000 criteria is becoming a competitive advantage for companies who have committed to ISO 9000 as a business strategy.

234

9. Engage a third-party certification agency. Plan a series of meetings to complete the certification process. The goal is to become registered by an agency.

10. When you receive your certificate of registration, plan a series of self-audits to assure that you remain in compliance.

For more information contact:

American Society for Quality Control
611 E. Wisconsin Ave.
Milwaukee, WI 53202
(414) 272-8575

National Center for Standards and Certification Information (NCSCI)
National Institute of Standards and Technology (NIST)
TRF Building, Room A163
Gaithersburg, MD 20899
(301) 975-4040

Office of EC Affairs
International Trade Administration
Room 3036
14th and Constitution Ave. S.W.
Washington, DC 20230
(202) 377-5276

U.S. Registration Accreditation Board (RAB)
611 E. Wisconsin Ave.
Milwaukee, WI 53202
(414) 272-8575

"Come, give us a taste of your quality."

William Shakespeare

235

CHAPTER 13

Customer Service
and Satisfaction

INTRODUCTION

Customer service and satisfaction are at the core of any
business. Throughout this manual are constant reminders to
begin with the customer. Customer requirements will drive
business strategy and serve as the ultimate measure of quality
in assessing your performance. The message here is simple
and profound: your customers sign your paycheck and make
it possible for you to open the door each new morning of the
business day.

Despite the driving competition in the world today, if you are
not afraid to listen to your customers and form partnerships
with them and your suppliers to deliver the highest quality for
the "best cost" — then you do not have to fear the
marketplace. You will "make" the marketplace and become a
company others will want to benchmark for your total
commitment to your customer.

Juran says that customer satisfaction is achieved when
products respond to customer needs and that customer
satisfaction is synonymous with product satisfaction, resulting
in more market share and increased sales income. Making
sure your organization is market-driven and not product-

*J.M. Juran defines
QUALITY as:*

*Product meets
customer needs
and is free of
deficiency.*

237

driven is a key point, however. Recognizing the difference between the two is essential to working with the positive direction of the source of energy. Market-driven companies are "pulled" into service by their customers; product-driven companies are "pushing" their goods into the marketplace.

The enviable position is to be "called upon" to deliver a service or product that stands out in a class of its own because somehow — despite the fact that you may make a million of them a year — that one single experience you did just for them. The telling tale during any audit or evaluation of customer service is told by how well the company measures the quality of its service to its customers.

What were the customer perceptions of the adequacy of the service? Is the data from customer feedback surveys reliable enough to plan improvements? If you work in a TQM company, you won't be scratching your head to find the answers to these questions. You will hear it straight from your customer over a cup of coffee one morning, and your internal design team will be ready to serve you to adapt the product to your customer's needs when you return to the office.

It is a whole new world in the marketplace. To some, it's faster and more competitive than ever; to others, it is a well-calibrated race with the best prizes going to those who collaborate with their ingenuity and their hearts. This is a race for the distance runners. The sprinters will discover their feats are no longer part of the contest.

"Inverting the Customer-Service Pyramid" on page 239 demonstrates vividly the shifts in positions that have occurred in the mind-set and operations of market-driven companies. Customers interface with the operating teams to say what they want from your company and how well you listened the last time. Customers serve on design teams, participate in user conferences and may become the most valid part of your market-distribution strategy. Companies that engage their customers in design, development and evaluation of their products and services are companies that are serious about achieving quality.

Notice how the entire senior team — CEO, COO, CFO — usually at the pinnacle of the diagram is now at the bottom. The role of the senior team is to support its managers in achieving business goals. The management team exists as a conduit to translate business goals into the functional output of the operating teams. Management exists to coach and help employees solve problems to deliver high-quality goods and services to customers at the best cost. The inverted pyramid illustrates this clearly.

INVERTING THE CUSTOMER-SERVICE PYRAMID

Get Close to the Customer

It is essential that employees see their work through the eyes of their customers and know how they actually use the products and experience the services provided for them. Employees will gain greater appreciation of the customer's needs and new insight into how best to respond to those needs. The inverted pyramid demonstrates how management must support the workers in serving the customers in optimal ways. Tom Peters became a management guru by adopting the role of Paul Revere, carrying the message of the inverted pyramid from coast to coast throughout the past decade.

How Some Companies Are Inverting the Pyramid

1. Site visits to customers where employees see the customers actually using the company's products. The formal process for this is called "quality mapping."

2. Videotape replay of customers using products and receiving services that employees produce.

3. More site visits to open communication with customers throughout an organization to listen for actual experience of individuals in the customer user chain.

4. Access to company products by employees to experience products from personal use — company support for discount-purchase plans.

> *"Trees die from the top."*
>
> **Peter F. Drucker**

239

5. Customer interface on project teams to produce product/service from concept and design through delivery.

6. User conferences.

What Is Service Quality?

Total Quality Management requires the systematic integration of:

- Customer Service
- Continuous Quality Improvement
- Organizational Development

Lasting Service and Quality Improvement require the integrated effort and involvement of everyone — suppliers, frontline performers, management and customers. TQM companies are continually checking their strategies and assessing themselves in all three areas.

Customer Service — In an increasingly crowded marketplace, Tom Peters explains "service added" is the competitive advantage. He points out the following:

1. Deliver service from the customer's standpoint. Focus on perfecting response to requirements and then move toward the "outer rings" of Service Quality models — where enhanced, "value-added" service is the new requirement.

2. View each customer as a lifetime customer who brings family and friends.

3. Pay attention to the intangible attributes of the service or product; design support systems and training programs to achieve outstanding, world-class customer service.

4. Get routine feedback on customer experience and perception and contrast with earlier measures of customer satisfaction, as well as the internal perceptions and experience of employees.

Continuous Quality Improvement — Commitment to continuous quality improvement is a full-time job. A TQM company requires:

1. Suppliers to become qualified through a certification program.

2. Senior management to invest fully and provide the tools necessary for employees to be effective in a TQM environment. Commit to strategic vision and leadership.

3. Managers to excel in their new roles of "coach," "teacher," "mentor," "resource developer" and "entrepreneur."

4. Employees to respond to customer needs with increased precision achieved through quality-improvement initiatives and programs; participate in new learning.

Organizational Development (OD) — As companies shift toward the new paradigm of how organizations operate today, many are realizing that it takes more than "talk" to create a culture change. To learn how to "walk the talk," companies are catching on that, unlike many other adjustments to American management theory and strategy, TQM has far less to do with structure and a great deal more to do with style and process.

Everyone needs to learn a new way of "being" and communicating. Some skeptics may wonder why all this is necessary; how does OD relate to customer service? Merely look at the marketplace to see change in customers, competitors, suppliers and employees. Shifting demographics create a need for cultural diversity and language programs just to speak with one another and know a bit about someone's orientation. Financial performance indicators make one conclude that a dramatic change is occurring in business and people must take greater responsibility and learn new skills to deal with rapid change and ever-improving technology. (Review some of the characteristics in the paradigm shifts in Chapter 9 to bring more of the current situation into full view.)

> *"If you take a comprehensive approach to TQM, you will succeed. If you do not, you will fail."*
>
> *David K. Carr*

The integration effort is a continuous process of informing, educating, measuring and assessing the experience of people throughout the customer-supplier chain.

TQM companies must commit to the following OD principles:

1. OD is an interactive and ongoing process which equips people to adapt to and lead change by learning new ways of relating to one another and expanding their interpersonal and analytic abilities.

2. OD is based on systems theory: when conditions in the external environment shift, so do the internal ones.

3. OD is a form of applied behavioral social science and relies on experience-based learning, a high level of group dynamics, data-based problem-solving and goal-setting and planning as routine activities to become more effective in processing change.

4. OD comprises these major operational components:

   — Diagnostic
   — Intervention
   — Process maintenance

Quality Awareness

The integration effort is a continuous process of informing, educating, measuring and assessing the experience of people throughout the customer-supplier chain. Dynamic interconnections with many people in that chain will serve you well in providing depth of understanding, accuracy of interpretation, commitment to problem-solving and a penchant for creating the best solutions to the most difficult problems.

To optimize the value of the customer-supplier chain, apply these foundation principles:

- Quality begins and ends with the customer.

  — To build a real quality advantage, everyone in the provider company needs to learn about their customers — who they are, why they use the products/services and how to keep them satisfied. First, last and always — customer requirements are the only true measure of quality. If you do nothing else this year, increase the ways and frequency of customer interface for employees from throughout the company. Send everyone "out to play" in the customer's playground and each person will return knowing a lot more about the "game" and how to make the next moves.

- Quality in the internal and external customer-supplier chain is the key determinant of quality for the end or "ultimate" customer.

  — Quality at the source requires that people at the nearest point of experience in a process or system be fully trained to run, measure and evaluate those systems and processes. A responsive attitude among co-workers and managers will create a willing tone for the company to function as a "learning organization" where people are not waiting to read tomorrow's news — they are creating it today. Seek out and listen to people within the system who possess "constructive dissatisfaction." They believe a "better way" exists; turn them loose and they will find it. The workers who challenge the status quo the most are our hope for the future.

Changing our work environment to support our customers, wherever they may be.

BENEFITS THROUGHOUT THE CUSTOMER-SUPPLIER CHAIN

Service Quality and TQM share an intense focus on customer requirements, service and satisfaction. They foster an internal environment that solicits and rewards creativity, innovation, risk-taking, communication and learning. Strategic Human Resources Management (SHRM) is at the heart of Service Quality and TQM. Internal and external suppliers and customers will be affected all along the chain.

CUSTOMER-SUPPLIER CHAIN

Benefits for external customers:

- Greater focus on their needs and specialized requirements
- Recipients of value-added services
- Increased partnership opportunities
- Improved quality in products, services, processes
- Reduced costs
- Greater reliability, dependability, adaptability
- Accessible communication through more frequent and informal interface
- Greater involvement in the planning and designing stages of requesting certain products and services

Benefits for internal customers:

- Greater support for continuous improvement
- Empowerment of employees to have greater responsibility for planning, problem-solving, decision-making, measuring and evaluating
- Predisposed, collaborative culture, encouraging trust and open communication
- Learning opportunities to enhance professional skills, individual and group achievements, and interpersonal understanding
- Expanded capacity for better success in the marketplace
- Expanded commitment to R&D

Benefits for highly rated Service Quality companies:

- Increased recognition and appreciation from current customers for company-wide quality performance and customer-friendly culture
- Enhanced Service Quality reputation attractive to new customers
- Better product-introduction success rates (ahead of the competition and in shortened development cycles)
- Better financial stability
- Expanded network of "troubleshooters" driving baselines to higher standards of excellence

One wonders why anyone would resist working for or with a highly rated Service Quality company, unless one would not want to become part of a TQM culture where:

- Expectations are high
- Open communication is the norm
- Customers are the reason the company is in business

People who are not ready to commit and produce their best may not be ready to join such companies.

> *"I have become a fanatic about quantifying but a new sort of quantifying ... the 'Soft Stuff' — quality service, customer linkups, innovation, organizational structure, people involvement."*
>
> *Tom Peters*

IMPLEMENTATION OF TQM SERVICE QUALITY CULTURE

Review the Implementation Diagram on the facing page to see how the principles and strategies of Total Quality Management (TQM) and Service Quality are represented in the framework for leading and processing change within an organization. The diagram provides a graphic representation of how to take an organization through a comprehensive transition.

Implementation is:

1. Driven by a vision of the future

2. Informed with analysis of present and past experience (surveys)

3. Guided by shared values that enable a willing culture

4. Infused with new interpersonal skills through a customized SHRM program

5. Supported by aligned strategies, systems and processes

6. Networked by the deployment of various responsibilities, a reporting schema and a structure through which to operate

> *"The secret to preparing for success is no secret at all."*
>
> ***Robb E. Dalton***

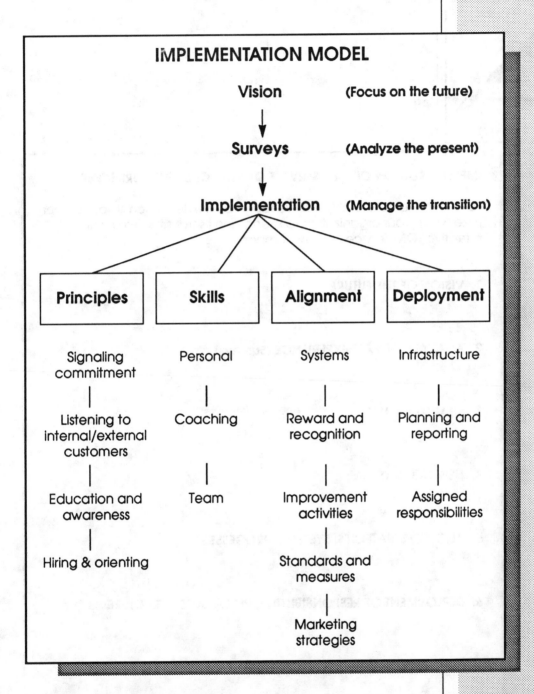

IMPLEMENTATION MODEL

Vision   (Focus on the future)

Surveys   (Analyze the present)

Implementation   (Manage the transition)

| Principles | Skills | Alignment | Deployment |

Signaling commitment | Personal | Systems | Infrastructure

Listening to internal/external customers | Coaching | Reward and recognition | Planning and reporting

Education and awareness | Team | Improvement activities | Assigned responsibilities

Hiring & orienting | | Standards and measures |

| | | Marketing strategies |

Source: *Service/Quality Academy, The Achieve Group, Inc., 8/91*

247

IMPLEMENTATION OF TQM SERVICE QUALITY CULTURE WORKSHEET

Following the outline of the six variables below, list action steps you can take within your organization to strengthen its transition to a highly effective TQM Service Quality company.

1. VISION OF THE FUTURE

2. ANALYSIS OF PAST EXPERIENCE (Surveys)

3. SHARED VALUES

4. NEW SKILLS (SHRM)

5. ALIGNED STRATEGIES, SYSTEMS, PROCESSES

6. DEPLOYMENT OF RESPONSIBILITIES, REPORTAGE, STRUCTURE

QUALITY FUNCTION DEPLOYMENT (QFD)

Competitive Edge for Customer Satisfaction

In Japan, company-wide quality control is characterized by a philosophy, a specification and a mechanism to deploy customer desires vertically and horizontally throughout the company. The mechanism has been named Company-Wide Quality Control (CWQC). The main objective of CWQC is to bring products to market faster than the competition with lower cost and improved quality — guided by precise input related to customer requirements. The vehicle for achieving this is called Quality Function Deployment (QFD). Translate this as one "sure bet" of a competitive market strategy.

Mitsubishi began QFD in Japan in 1972, but it took until 1983 before U.S. companies began to be exposed to it. Ford is the recognized QFD leader in the United States today. Ford considers its QFD programs "proprietary information" because it gives the company a real competitive edge.

Quality Function Deployment is an overall concept that provides a means of translating technical requirements for each stage of product development and production. Marketing strategies, planning, product design and engineering, evaluation, production process development, production and sales are part of QFD.

Key concepts associated with QFD are:

- The voice of the customer — customer requirements expressed in their own terms.

- Counterpart characteristics — an expression of the voice of the customer in technical language that specifies customer-required quality; counterpart characteristics are critical to final product control.

- Product Quality Deployment (PQD) — activities needed to translate the voice of the customer into counterpart characteristics.

> **Rule #1:**
>
> *The customer is always right.*
>
> **Rule #2:**
>
> *If the customer is ever wrong, reread rule #1.*

249

- Deployment of the Quality Function — activities needed to assure that customer-required quality is achieved; the assignment of specific quality responsibilities to specific departments or teams.

- Quality Tables — a series of matrices to translate the voice of the customer into final product control characteristics.

Benefits of Quality Function Development

The customer's voice has been driving quality in Japanese companies for many years; in the United States, the CEO's voice has prevailed. Japanese companies take a longer time planning the program because of QFD, where they take plenty of time to capture "the voice of the customer" in precise and technical terms early in the process; this saves many dollars and hours later on. For companies who can perfect QFD, the benefits are great:

- Product objectives based on customer requirements are interpreted accurately at subsequent stages.

- Particular marketing strategies or "sales points" do not become lost or blurred during the translation process from marketing through planning and on to execution.

- Important production control points are not overlooked — everything necessary to achieve the desired outcome is understood and in place.

- Tremendous efficiency is achieved because misinterpretations — of program objectives, marketing strategy and critical control points — and the need for change are minimized.

Determining Customer Satisfaction

Just as customer requirements drive quality in the very beginning of the relationship with the client, they remain the driving force throughout the design, development and delivery of the product or service. How well a company meets those customer requirements may be the clearest way to assess customer satisfaction.

Customer satisfaction should not be surveyed at the end; there is no end. Customers need to give feedback constantly to assure the best possible fulfillment of their requirements. There are many ways to work closely with the customer throughout the process:

- Customer representative on design & development team
- Employee exchange program to deepen understanding of one another's companies, products, processes, quality issues and pressures
- Cross-over training program to learn an integrated system that will serve both companies
- Collaborative project team
- Customer representative as guest speaker
- On-site visit exchange
- Scheduled, periodic program-review meetings
- User conferences
- Collaborative problem-solving team to work on most critical deficiencies

Exercise

1. What other ideas do you have for obtaining customer feedback? What do you do that you find effective?

2. Reflect on a customer (internal or external) situation of yours that got away from you. Why did it happen? List the reasons only you believe there was a problem. Also, identify what you could do differently next time in a similar situation. Write down these ideas and consider them part of your "prevention" tool kit. Did you ever ask the customer to explain what went wrong?

Exercise

251

Factors to Consider in Determining Customer Requirements

Two techniques can assist in the process of determining customer requirements. Customer requirements define the quality of your product or service. The two techniques are the quality-dimension development process, which involves people closely linked to the service or product, and the critical-incidents technique, which involves customers who experienced a critical incident that influenced them either positively or negatively.

The quality-dimension development process engages people familiar with the needs of the customer and the function and purpose of the product. These people are responsible for determining the quality dimensions, definitions of the quality dimensions and specific examples of each dimension.

The critical-incidents approach involves obtaining information from customers about an actual experience where they believe a critical incident defined either good or bad aspects of the product. These incidents define the satisfaction items, which in turn define the customer requirements.

Scan the chart on the facing page describing steps to follow when determining customer requirements by either of these methods.

PROCEDURES FOR ESTABLISHING CUSTOMER REQUIREMENTS

Nothing is more central to the success of a business than meeting customer requirements. Requirements cannot be met without first establishing them with your customers. Here is a process outline of how to establish customer requirements that reflect the critical quality dimension that customers value.

QUALITY-DIMENSION DEVELOPMENT

STEPS	IMPORTANT POINTS
1. Create list of quality dimensions.	• Read professional and trade journals to obtain list of quality dimensions. • Generate list from personal experience.
2. Write definitions of each dimension.	• Definition can be in general terms.
3. Develop specific examples for each quality dimension.	• Examples should use specific adjectives reflecting the service or product. • Examples should include specific behaviors of the provider. • Examples should use declarative statements.

CRITICAL-INCIDENTS APPROACH

Steps	Important Points
1. Generate critical incidents.	• Interview customers.
	• Critical incidents should be specific examples of good or poor service or product quality.
	• Each critical incident reflects only one example.
2. Categorize critical incidents into clusters.	• Categorization is based on similarity in content of the incidents.
3. Write satisfaction items for each critical-incident cluster.	• Each satisfaction item should be a declarative statement.
	• Satisfaction items should be specific.
4. Categorize satisfaction items into clusters, each cluster representing a customer requirement.	• Categorization should be based on similarity of satisfaction items.
	• Customer requirement must reflect the content of satisfaction items.
5. Determine the quality of the categorization process.	• Two judges should do categorization steps.
	• Calculate agreement with both judges.
6. Determine the comprehensiveness of customer requirements.	• Remove 10% of the critical incidents before establishing customer requirements.
	• Determine whether the 10% can be placed into the customer requirements.

Bob E. Hayes, *Measuring Customer Satisfaction*, ASQC Quality Press, Milwaukee, WI, 1992, pp. 26-27.

GUIDELINES IN DEVELOPING CUSTOMER-SATISFACTION QUESTIONNAIRES

Customer-satisfaction questionnaires are a tool to provide feedback about how satisfied a customer is with the work that was done for him or her — or how well the work responded to the customer's requirements. The following guidelines will help you develop a Customer-Satisfaction Questionnaire.

CUSTOMER-SATISFACTION QUESTIONNAIRES

STEPS	IMPORTANT ISSUES
1. Generate items for questionnaire.	• Select items from satisfaction item list.
	• Write items based on satisfaction items.
2. Ensure items are written appropriately.	• Items should appear relevant to what you are trying to measure.
	• Items should be concise.
	• Items should be unambiguous.
	• Items should contain only one thought (items ask only one question).
	• Items should not contain double negatives.
3. Select the response format for items.	• Checklist format.
	• Likert-type format (1...2...3...4...5)

CUSTOMER-SATISFACTION QUESTIONNAIRES (continued)

STEPS	IMPORTANT ISSUES
4. Write an introduction to questionnaire.	• State the purpose of the questionnaire.
	• State instructions on how to complete the questionnaire.
5. Select representative sample of items.	• Items within each quality dimension should be similar in content to each other.
a. Could use judgmental item selection to select items	• Use multiple judges to select the items.
b. Could use mathematical item selection to select items	• Use aggregate correlations or group differences approach in selecting items.
	• Could also use factor analysis.
6. Evaluate the retained items.	• Calculate reliability of the scales within questionnaire.

Bob E. Hayes, *Measuring Customer Satisfaction*, ASQC Quality Press, Milwaukee, WI, 1992, pp. 26-27.

USES OF CUSTOMER-SATISFACTION QUESTIONNAIRES

Uses	Important Issues
1. Present current standing of customer satisfaction.	• Present means and standard deviations of specific items as well as overall scores of each dimension.
2. Identify important customer requirements.	• Use correlational analysis relating customer requirements to overall satisfaction scores.
3. Monitor satisfaction levels over time.	• Use control charting techniques. • Control chart method depends on type of response format you select (checklist-attribute data vs. Likert-type-variable data).
4. Provide organizational comparisons.	• Comparisons should be made of companies using same questionnaire. • Independent research firm could conduct comparisons.
5. Determine program effectiveness.	• Evaluate effect of training programs. • Conduct benchmarking studies.

Bob E. Hayes, *Measuring Customer Satisfaction*, ASQC Quality Press, Milwaukee, WI, 1992, pp. 26-27.

DEVELOPING YOUR OWN CUSTOMER-SERVICE
SATISFACTION QUESTIONNAIRE

1. Generate items.

2. Review and revise written items.

3. Determine response format.

4. Write introduction.

5. Evaluate items.

6. Revise questionnaire.

CHAPTER 14

Evaluation/Options for the Future

INTRODUCTION

As with measurement, where anything worth doing is worth measuring, any improvement process worth implementing is worth evaluating. People care about results. The investment to achieve a total-quality environment is not small, nor should the return be. The "Quality Story" — how well the improvement process is working — is one companies should be excited to find out about or tell.

Companies initially struggle with deciding whether they should commit the resources to a continuous-improvement process ...

"Can we afford to spend the money?"

"Can we spare the people for all that training? We have downsized so much, we really need people on the job."

"Our margins have been so slim, it is difficult to justify that we must spend money to control costs."

"TQM? That's just this year's latest buzzword for turning around the economy ..."

The resistance is understandable. The constraints are real. Pressures in the marketplace have made it very difficult for some industries to redistribute their dollars to seek the improvements they need. However, many who delay the commitment to tackle the job of quality and productivity improvement discover that they have an increasingly difficult time meeting their goals.

For those companies that commit their drive and their dollars, it is key that they take time to evaluate the results. The same is true for departments that embark on just one improvement process.

The thrust of improvement processes is to achieve "Best Cost" in meeting customer requirements. Evaluations of the many individual department and team efforts and evaluation of the company as a whole are useful to keep the company focused on its progress and where it continues to have problems.

This final chapter addresses how quality and evaluation are viewed and accomplished by companies who are traveling along the road of continuous improvement. Additionally, Chapter 14 provides a profile of several companies who have won the Baldrige Award. Their results speak for themselves. Finally, "Options for the Future" will help you and your company plan your next steps along your own road of continuous improvement. The journey may be difficult, but it is worth it.

> *"Until you implement a decision, it is not really a decision at all."*
>
> *Edward C. Schleh*

EVALUATION IS AN ONGOING PROCESS

Evaluation for TQM companies occurs in the true spirit of the continuous-improvement process. Evaluation isn't something one does at the end. There is no end! Evaluation is considered during the planning and design stages of each improvement strategy when criteria for success are established in the objectives.

From the beginning, people know how they will evaluate the new initiative. Companies and departments stay close to their own improvement methodology and routinely conduct reality tests to receive feedback from their markets, suppliers and employees. Continuous improvement requires that the "learning" from the evaluation be captured and reflected into the next steps of the process.

External Evaluation

Quality companies put themselves through external evaluation, where they are assessed against rigorous excellence criteria such as those utilized in the application and assessment process for the Malcolm Baldrige Award. By applying for various recognition awards, companies explain that their entire operation becomes very involved with understanding their own level of effectiveness and efficiency in meeting customer requirements. The application and evaluation process becomes an opportunity for the company to discover its strengths and weaknesses and to set goals for improvements it believes will reward both the customers and the bottom line.

Once a company goes through an extensive evaluation process such as the one for the Baldrige Award, the company can create its own process to monitor its progress on an ongoing basis. In Chapter 7, "TQM Organizational Readiness Assessment" provides an overview of the company and can be used repeatedly within the company to track improvements. The TQM Organizational Readiness Assessment process provides for evaluation of a company based on these main criteria: productivity and leadership, human resources excellence, productivity/quality results, customer orientation and results, and the impact on the community.

> *Evaluation is the journey of life.*

In Chapter 4, the "Vendor Performance Rating" reflects the areas of significance that GM values in certifying its suppliers as its business partners in serving the ultimate customer. The evaluation criteria provide guidelines for assessing quality and responsiveness to customers. Suppliers are assessed in the areas of management, effective human resources management, quality and quality control, responsiveness to needs, corrective action related to nonconformance issues, quality and control of subcontractors, cost and cost reduction, manufacturing and technology, among others.

Discover common quality themes among the companies presented here and see how ongoing internal and external evaluation will carry you along the road of continuous improvement and inform your company of its progress.

MALCOLM BALDRIGE NATIONAL QUALITY AWARD

The Malcolm Baldrige National Quality Award sets the standard for excellence for U.S. companies. Named for the former Secretary of Commerce, the award was established by an Act of Congress on January 6, 1987, to:

- Promote quality awareness

- Recognize quality achievements of U.S. companies

- Publicize successful quality strategies

The Secretary of Commerce and the National Institute of Standards and Technology are given responsibilities to develop and administer the Awards with cooperation and financial support from the private sector. As many as six companies can win each year. There are three award categories: manufacturing, services and small business.

Companies submit written applications, in which they respond to numerous questions that attempt to determine how well organized they are to promote a TQM environment. Some of the criteria in the application relate to factors such as leadership and values, information and analyses, strategic quality planning, human resources utilization, quality results (levels and improvements), quality assurance of products and services, and customer satisfaction.

The application process is rigorous and the key concepts used in the criteria reflect the total quality principles already described in this manual. After a Board of Examiners reviews the written applications, several candidates are selected for site visits and interviews. Applicants receive a written summary of strengths and areas for improvement in their total-quality management. Companies take two years or more preparing to apply for the award; most say they learned a lot about themselves in the preparation stages and gained improvements along the continuum of TQM readiness.

Malcolm Baldrige Award: Key Points for Evaluation

The following demonstrates the key areas in which companies are evaluated for the Malcolm Baldrige Award. U.S. companies that participate explain it is not the award itself that is the actual goal, although the recognition is reassuring and often means increased revenues. Companies report a newfound commitment and precision among their employees when they pull together to prepare for the Baldrige evaluation. Just beginning the journey serves as a tonic for many companies and employees.

Leadership

- Senior-management involvement
- Quality values
- Management system
- Public responsibility

Information Analysis

- Scope of information and data
- Data management
- Analysis and use of data

> *"Be not afraid of greatness: some are born great, some achieve greatness, and some have greatness thrust upon them."*
>
> **William Shakespeare**

> *Winners expect to win. Life is a self-fulfilling prophecy.*

263

Strategic Quality Planning

- Planning process
- Plans for quality leadership benchmarking
- Priorities

Human Resource Utilization

- Management
- Employee involvement
- Education and training
- Employee recognition
- Quality of work life

Quality Assurance

- Design and introduction of products and services
- Operation of processes
- Measurements and standards
- Audit
- Documentation
- Business processes
- External providers of goods and services

Quality Results

- Quality of products and services
- Competitive comparison
- Operational and business process quality improvement
- Supplier quality improvement

Customer Satisfaction

- Knowledge of customer requirements and expectations
- Customer relationship management
- Commitment
- Complaint management
- Customer satisfaction determination
- Customer satisfaction trends

"What I expect out of all employees is that they do their utmost to see we deliver what we told our customers we'd do 100% of the time."

Fred Smith, CEO Federal Express MBNQA — Quality Service

FOR MORE INFORMATION ABOUT THE BALDRIGE AWARD:

Malcolm Baldrige National Quality Award
National Institute of Standards and Technology
Administration Building, Room A537
Gaithersburg, MD 20899
Telephone (301) 975-2036
FAX (301) 948-3716

OPTIONS FOR THE FUTURE

Organizations that are committed to improving their productivity and pursuing a Total Quality Improvement Strategy often want to know where to start. People learn in different ways, but it is true that when different learning modes are combined, retention and application are higher.

Listen to Juran and Deming on tape; try to catch Phil Crosby in lecture. List your favorite companies with whom you may want to benchmark. Attend seminars. Who else in your business is already doing some of these things?

You can proceed in logical ways when you have gained enough up-front input. Who within the company will be the dynamos for the change process? Where will the opposition come from? Who do you need to get behind this initiative? Who are your mentors and soul mates? You will need them. The TQM road is a long one, although worth it.

As with any problem-solving process, the first place to start is with identifying the symptoms. This may be more difficult than one might guess. A needs assessment may be a first step. In investigating for TQM readiness — information is collected from everyone through surveys, individual and small group interviews, work meetings and planning sessions.

A diagnosis is made after an informed understanding of the current status of the company is obtained. Findings are presented to an organization and much discussion occurs. The top team and the second tier are interviewed very carefully to get a clear reading of individual experience.

> *"If you want to know a company's values, just look at its annual report."*
>
> *John Stewart*

265

Various approaches and interventions are discussed. Who needs coaching? What will the TQM steering committee be asked to do? How does one calm the misgivings of certain individuals? What needs to be done first? This last question is repeated regularly by TQM companies — get used to it!

Developing a plan for sustained commitment is critical to the success of TQM. The early stages provoke high anxiety among everyone. People are trying to find out if TQM will be worth it. Leadership has to be clear and supportive.

A steering committee is formed. Usually, the senior core team is represented heavily, and others are pulled in from the second and third tier who have the interest and the ability to participate in shaping a change process. They receive an orientation in TQM and usually take a refresher course in problem-solving and how to work in teams.

The committee works on developing its plan for action. An assessment is made of other training and resource needs that the group has. Usually, one process is selected as a pilot for improvement. People are selected to work within that process. Data-analysis needs are determined and tools are provided. The objectives and goals of the pilot are clarified and a cross-functional process maps out a plan and strategy.

The organization will learn from the pilot and the early experiences of the team as they begin to benchmark and set their sights on improvement. The organization will have to be prepared to invest heavily in training. TQM is intensive in its high participation of people. In order for the people to do well and experience success, they will need the skills and tools to change how they work together and apply new technical methods.

Measurement systems are important to gauge the improvements that are made and to understand how they occurred. Operational training, planning, and ongoing development and linkages with all new process-improvement teams are pivotal in creating the collaborations necessary to make TQM work. Ongoing evaluation continues to strengthen everyone's understanding of what they are doing in the continuous-improvement process and what success they are having.

> "Quality is our only form of patent protection."
>
> James Robinson
> CEO — Am Ex

As the company experiences success with improvement teams, the energy and enthusiasm will build. More people will want to get involved. There will be a new air to breathe and that air is called Quality. Quality with a common purpose will extend to include suppliers as partners.

Policy changes and new incentives will be required. Employee and customer feedback surveys will provide impressions and ideas to the organization as it advances along the TQM model. What was once a big mystery will become the organization's norm. Quality and productivity go hand in hand. People like things to work. You can make things work by collaborating in teams focused on improvements throughout your company. The road of continuous improvement never ends. Its quality rewards of satisfied customers, innovative products and challenging work will make it worth your journey.

"Reasserting our leadership position will require a firm commitment to TQM and the principle of continuous improvement."

President George Bush

267

COMMON TERMS

Acceptable Quality Level (AQL)

The maximum percent defective (or maximum number of defects per 100 units) that, for purposes of acceptance sampling, can be considered satisfactory as a process average.

Audit

An independent review conducted to compare some aspect of performance with the standard for that performance.

Baldrige, Malcolm Quality Award

The coveted quality award named after the late Malcolm Baldrige, Secretary of Commerce. It recognizes organizations with the best quality products and services.

Boundary

The beginning or end point in the portion of a process from a Supplier to a Customer that will be the focus of a process-improvement effort.

Acceptable Quality Level (AQL)

Audit

Baldrige, Malcolm Quality Award

Boundary

Brainstorming

*Cause-and-Effect
Diagram*

Center Line

Check Sheet

*Common-Cause
System of
Variation*

*Common-Cause
Variation*

*Company-Wide
Quality Control
(CWQC)*

Brainstorming

A group decision-making technique designed to generate a large number of creative ideas through an interactive process. Brainstorming is used to generate alternative ideas to be considered in making decisions.

Cause-and-Effect Diagram

See Ishikawa Diagram.

Center Line

The line on a control chart that represents the average (mean or median) value of items being plotted.

Check Sheet

A data-collection form consisting of multiple categories. Each category has an operational definition and can be checked off as it occurs. Properly designed, the Check Sheet helps to summarize data, which is often displayed in a Pareto Chart.

Common-Cause System of Variation

The collection of variables that produce common variation and the interaction of those variables.

Common-Cause Variation

Variation is a process that is caused by the process itself and is produced by interactions of variables of that process.

Company-Wide Quality Control (CWQC)

Puts the responsibility for quality throughout all divisions, departments and teams of a quality company. CWQC is achieved when a company's vision, mission and goal are communicated throughout the organization and people are trained to work together to achieve the best results at the least cost to the customer. (See Quality Function Deployment [QFD]).

Competitive Benchmarking

A continuous process that measures an organization's performance against the "best of the best" in a specific industry. (See World Class Benchmarking.)

Conformance

Represents the capability of an organization through its employees, departments/teams, divisions and suppliers to meet customer requirements.

Control Chart

A display of data in the order that they occur with statistically determined upper and lower limits of expected common-cause variation. It is used to indicate special causes of process variation, to monitor a process for maintenance and to determine whether process changes have had the desired quality effect. It is one of the basic tools of Total Quality Management.

Control Limits

Expected limits of common-cause variation. Often they are referred to as upper and lower control limits. They are not specification or tolerance limits.

Cost of Quality/Poor Quality

The costs associated with achieving quality can be tracked while the costs associated with poor quality are viewed as an unknowable number. Streamlining a work process through the upgrading of new technology and training of the people to use it equates to an actual dollar expenditure.

Culture

Authoritarian Culture

An organizational culture characterized by the holding of all power (decision-making and information) at the top of the organization. The authoritarian organization seeks to maintain the status quo and forces workers to conform, never question or give feedback, play politics and wait for orders.

Competitive Benchmarking

Conformance

Control Chart

Control Limits

Cost of Quality/Poor Quality

Culture

271

Customer

*Customer-
Friendly Systems*

Data Collection

*Ishikawa
Diagram*

Just-in-Time (JIT)

Collaborative Culture

An organizational culture characterized by a shared vision, shared leadership, empowered workers, cooperation among organization units as they work to improve processes, a high degree of openness to feedback and data, and optimization of the organizational whole vs. its many parts.

Customer

The receiver of an output process, either internal or external. A customer could be a department, a person, a company, etc.

Customer-Friendly Systems

Procedures and policies that make it easy for customers to access and interact with an organization.

Data Collection

Gathering facts on how a process works and/or how a process is working from the customer's point of view. All data collection is driven by knowledge of the process and guided by statistical principles.

Ishikawa Diagram

A graphic tool used to explore and display all factors that may influence or cause a given outcome. One of the basic tools of TQM. (Also known as a Cause-and-Effect or Fishbone Diagram.)

Just-in-Time (JIT)

A manufacturing process where all of the activities take place so that only the required material is at the necessary place at the necessary time. (Also called Stockless Production.)

Key Process Variable (KPV)

A component of the process that has a cause-and-effect relationship of sufficient magnitude with the Key Quality Characteristic (KQC). Manipulation and control of the KPV will reduce variation of the KQC and/or change its level.

Key Quality Characteristics (KQC)

The most important quality characteristics. KQCs must be operationally defined by combining knowledge of the customer with knowledge of the process. KQCs are measured to understand the actual performance of the process.

Macro Process

A process that cuts across departmental, business or divisional boundaries.

Micro Process

A process within a department's or group's jurisdiction.

Median

In a series of numbers, the median is the number that has at least half the values greater than or equal to it and at least half of them less than or equal to it.

Key Process Variable (KPV)

Key Quality Characteristics (KQC)

Macro Process

Micro Process

Median

Meeting Process

Multiple Voting

Nominal Group Technique

Nonconformance

Operational Definition

Meeting Process

A defined method for conducting meetings that includes specific roles and responsibilities for a team leader, a timekeeper, team members and a facilitator. The steps include:

1) Clarify the objective
2) Review roles
3) Review the agenda
4) Work through the agenda items
5) Review the meeting record
6) Plan the agenda and methods
7) Evaluate

Multiple Voting

A group decision-making technique designed to reduce a long list to a few ideas.

Nominal Group Technique

A group-process technique designed to generate a large number of ideas efficiently through input from individual group members.

Nonconformance

Reflects the inability of an organization to satisfy customer requirements.

Operational Definition

A description of quantifiable terms of what to measure and the steps to follow to measure it consistently. Deming has suggested that a good operational definition include:

1) A criterion to be applied
2) A way to determine whether the criterion is satisfied
3) A way to interpret the results of the test

An operational definition is developed for each KQC or process variable before data is collected.

274

Opportunity Statement

A concise description of a process in need of improvement, its boundaries and the general area of concern where a quality improvement team should begin its efforts.

Outcome (Benefit)

The degree to which outputs meet the need and expectations of the Customer.

Owner

The person who has or is given the responsibility and authority to lead the continuing improvement of a process. Process ownership is a designation made by leaders of organizations and depends on the boundaries of the process.

Paradigm Shift

A point in time when the knowledge or structure that underlies a science or discipline changes in such a fundamental way that the beliefs and behavior of the people involved in the science or discipline are changed.

Pareto Chart

A bar graph used to arrange information in such a way that priorities for process improvement can be established. It displays the relative importance of data and is used to direct efforts to the biggest improvement opportunity by highlighting the vital few in contrast to the many others.

Present State

In a force field analysis, the description of an organization as it currently exists. It includes what happens in the organization, both formally and informally.

Opportunity Statement

Outcome (Benefit)

Owner

Paradigm Shift

Pareto Chart

Present State

275

Process

A series of actions that repeatedly come together to transform inputs to outputs. The combination of people, machines and equipment, raw materials, methods and environment that produces a given product or service.

Process Capability

The normal behavior of a process when operating in the statistical control; the minimum variation achievable after all causes of variation have been eliminated.

Process Control

The gathering of data about a process and the establishment of a feedback loop to prevent the manufacture of nonconforming products. (See Statistical Process Control.)

Process Improvement

The continuous endeavor to learn about all aspects of a process and to use this knowledge to change the process to reduce variation and complexity and to improve customer judgments of quality. Process improvement begins by understanding how customers judge quality, how processes work and how understanding the variation in those processes can lead to wise management action.

Process Variation

The spread of process output over time. There is variation in every process, and all variation is caused. The causes are two types: special or common. A process can have both types of variation at the same time or only common cause variation. The management action necessary to improve the process is very different in each situation.

Quality

One hundred percent conformance to customer needs and wants.

Quality Assurance

Designing a product or service so well that quality is inevitable.

Quality Characteristics

Characteristics of the output of a process that are important to the customer. The identification of quality characteristics requires knowledge of customer needs and expectations.

Quality Circle

A process to improve productivity and strengthen quality initiatives around process improvement using employees from all parts of the organization as a whole.

Quality Function Deployment (QFD)

A concept to educate those responsible for delivering quality in both functions and processes, as well as in the final products, by making quality operational at the source.

Quality Improvement Team

A specially constituted group, usually five to eight people, chosen to address a specific opportunity for improvement. Consists of those people who have regular contact with the process.

Quality Inspection

Usually consists of three stages: sampling, measuring and sorting. While many organizations rely on inspection to improve quality, the better way is to design quality into the product or service — to improve the process. This may include inspections as a means of data gathering.

Quality Assurance

Quality Characteristics

Quality Circle

Quality Function Deployment (QFD)

Quality Improvement Team

Quality Inspection

Rework

> The act of doing something again because it was not done right the first time. It can occur for a variety of reasons, including insufficient planning, failure of a customer to specify the needed input and failure of a supplier to provide a consistently high-quality output.

Run

> A point or a consecutive number of points that are above or below the central line in a run chart. Too long a run or too many or too few runs can be evidence of the existence of special causes of variation.

Run Chart

> A display of data in the order they occur. Run charts display Process Variation and can be used to indicate special causes of Process Variation in the form of trends, shifts and other non-random patterns.

Statistical Process Control

> A system of measuring variance in production systems.

Statistical Thinking for Process Improvement

> A data-driven method for decision-making based primarily on an understanding of Process Variation. It results in wise management actions that contribute to the continuous improvement of quality.

Supplier

> The party or entity responsible for input to a process. A supplier could be a person, a department, a company, etc.

Tampering

> Taking action without taking into account the difference between special and common-cause variation.

Team Leader

> A person designated to lead the Quality Improvement Team.

Teams

Cross-functional

A group, usually of five to eight people from two or more areas of an organization, that addresses an issue that impacts the operations of each area.

Functional

A group of five to eight people addressing an issue where any recommended changes would probably not affect people outside the group's specific area.

Total Quality Control (TQC)

Effort expended by a company to achieve the quality its customers demand.

Total Quality Management Tools

A group of techniques and charts used to collect, organize, display and evaluate knowledge about a process. Brainstorming, Flow Chart, Cause-and-Effect Diagram, Check Sheet, Pareto Chart, Run Chart and Control Chart are examples of these tools.

Transformation

A major organizational change from present state to a new/preferred state.

Transition Period

A description of the time when an organization is visibly moving from the old way toward a new way. During this time employee attitudes and behaviors range from excitement and industriousness to confusion and resistance. The support for change is building. New leaders emerge, champions of change come forward and confusion over roles begins to clear.

Teams

Total Quality Control (TQC)

Total Quality Management Tools

Transformation

Transition Period

279

Ultimate Customer

The person or unit who receives the output from a series of processes and for whom the processes are designed. Without the ultimate customer, there would be no need for the intermediate process to exist.

Vision Statement

A summary of an organization's performance expectations that will lead it to future success. The statement should be clear, measurable, have a specific time frame, clarify anticipated accomplishments, project the "team" into the future and be written briefly in paragraph form.

World-Class Benchmarking

The continuous process of measuring products, services or practices against world leaders.

Zero Defects

This concept of a defect-free product has value as a long-range objective, since it suggests the need for never-ending improvement. The concept rejects the idea that we can relax our efforts short of perfection.

I NDEX

A

Activities That Affect Costs in a Quality System Checklist, 202-05
average/mean, 215

B

Baldrige, Malcolm, National Quality Award, 17, 18, 21, 23, 119, 261, 262-65
barriers, 132-39
   removing, 135
   See also: Force Field Analysis
         resistance
Bell Labs, 65
benchmarking, 186-90
Benchmarking Checklist, 188-89
benefits of TQM to companies, 64
"Best Cost," 37, 40
brainstorming, 168-69
Business Planning Worksheet, 195-96

C

D